CEDAC®

A Tool for Continuous Systematic Improvement

Dr. Ryuji Fukuda

Productivity Press
CAMBRIDGE, MASSACHUSETTS
NORWALK, CONNECTICUT

CEDAC®

A Tool for Continuous Systematic Improvement

Originally published as CEDAC® *shisutemu doonyuu tekisuto*, copyright © 1986 by Japan Business Report Company, Ltd, Tokyo.

English translation copyright © 1989 by Productivity, Inc.

CEDAC is a registered trademark of Productivity, Inc.

Productivity Press
P.O. Box 3007
Cambridge, MA 02140
(617) 497-5146

or

Productivity, Inc.
101 Merritt 7 Corporate Park
Norwalk, CT 06851
(203) 846-3777

Library of Congress Catalog Card Number: 89-43210
ISBN: 0-915299-26-7

Book design by Rudra Press
Cover design by Dick Hannus
Typeset by Rudra Press, Cambridge, MA
Printed and bound by Arcata/Halliday
Printed in the United States of America

Library of Congress Cataloging-in-Publication Data

Fukuda, Ryuji, 1928-
  CEDAC *shisutemu donyu tekisuto.*   English
  CEDAC: a tool for continuous systematic improvement/by Ryuji Fukuda.
      p. cm.
  Translation of: CEDAC shisutemu donyu tekisuto.
  ISBN 0-915299-26-7
  1. Production management   I. Title
TS155.F7713   1990
658.5 — dc20   89-43210
                                                                                          CIP

91 92 10 9 8 7 6 5 4 3 2

Table of Contents

List of Figures

Publisher's Foreword

In the mid-1970s, one of Japan's most successful manufacturing companies, Sumitomo Electric, decided to expand into the international market. As part of that decision, Sumitomo saw the need for improving its standard operating procedures, an important step in setting up new facilities in other countries and capturing their markets. Sumitomo realized that reliable methods were a major guarantee that it could produce the same high quality in a foreign workplace that it produced in Japan. It also realized the need for the involvement of everyone in the workforce if procedures were to be truly effective and problems eliminated.

As a result, Sumitomo asked Dr. Ryuji Fukuda to create a method for developing effective standard procedures. Dr. Fukuda, who had begun his distinguished career in 1954 as an engineering graduate from Kyoto University, had worked at Sumitomo for nearly 20 years in a variety of quality and productivity positions. He had some ideas about how to develop a comprehensive improvement approach that would harness the power of the workforce for solving problems and developing more effective standards, and he was eager to get started.

He asked a group of Sumitomo volunteers to pick a workplace problem and develop and test his own approach to solving it. Meeting once a month, the study group grew to over 100 members and, after a year of research, CEDAC was born: a powerful tool for continuous systematic improvement.

Sumitomo piloted CEDAC in its 40 plants between 1976 and 1979. The 350 CEDAC projects that resulted produced benefits that amazed everyone, including Dr. Fukuda and his study group. In some cases, the defect rate dropped by over 60% in the first three months of projects. In fact, the outcomes were so unexpected that Dr. Fukuda decided to research the phenomenon. The paper he published on that research won the 1978 Nikai Award, an adjunct to the Deming Award competition. (Portions of that paper are published here in the Appendix.)

In 1982, I met Dr. Fukuda while leading an executive study mission to Japan and our friendship and business relationship began with the publication of his book *Managerial Engineering*, a vivid description of the origins of CEDAC and other useful insights into quality and productivity improvement.

The power of continuous improvement, the simplicity of the CEDAC approach, and the benefits it had produced for Sumitomo impressed me. I decided to make CEDAC more widely available to U.S. business and industry. In 1984, I hired Dr. Gwendolyn Galsworth for the express purpose of developing CEDAC into a comprehensive tool that American companies could understand, appreciate, and successfully implement.

Dr. Galsworth, Dr. Derek Kotze, and their colleagues have worked on the development of CEDAC, conferring frequently with Dr. Fukuda, and piloted the

American version of CEDAC in a variety of settings. What has resulted is a methodology that works, reliably and powerfully, to promote and establish a process of systematic continuous improvement in the workplace as it involves the entire workforce.

This workbook introduces the reader to the main elements of the CEDAC system that Dr. Fukuda has used with many clients around the world, from Mitsubishi Heavy Industries to Fiat and SONY in both North America and Europe. The handbook provides a useful explanation of window analysis as a tool for problem identification as well as a description of the CEDAC Diagram procedure. CEDAC can be applied to very sophisticated problems and complex transactions and has been used with great success, in partnership with our training staff, by Weyerhauser, Pratt & Whitney, GM of Canada, ITT Aerospace, and many others.

CEDAC continues to have tremendous success all over the United States, Canada, Europe, Australia, and most recently India. One of the most amazing parts of the CEDAC story is that the CEDAC implementations outside Japan have enjoyed success profiles similar to that of the Sumitomo pilot in the 1970s — achieving a rapid drop in defects, problems, and waste.

We at Productivity Press are pleased to offer this CEDAC workbook, to support continuous systematic improvement in every workplace environment. As a companion volume to *Managerial Engineering* this concise guide will help to clarify the many methods of the CEDAC System, including the CEDAC Diagram. As an introduction to the CEDAC System, it will get you started in the ever-evolving and expanding adventure of continuous improvement management and employee involvement.

With much gratitude we acknowledge Dr. Ryuji Fukuda's seminal work in developing improvement methodologies and revolutionary philosophy of management. Thanks also to Noriko Hosoyamada for retranslating and updating much of this book according to Dr. Fukuda's instructions, to Diane Asay for editing the manuscript, to Dick Hannus for the cover design, and to David Lennon and the staff of Rudra Press for their fine work in producing this attractive and useful workbook.

Norman Bodek
Publisher

Author's Preface

Special Features of the CEDAC System

- Application of the CEDAC system vitalizes improvement activities and promotes steady progress toward positive results.
- The CEDAC System establishes an atmosphere of "continuous improvement." It enables people to make full use of their accumulated knowledge and experience of technology and managerial engineering. It eliminates a "shopping around" environment, where people pursue one new management technique after another without perfecting any. The CEDAC system does not replace existing techniques but integrates and supplements them.
- The CEDAC system changes organization culture. Needed most for this change is day-to-day leadership in improvement activities by group leaders, foremen, supervisors, managers, and senior managers. The CEDAC system provides genuine assistance to those people.
- The CEDAC System can be used easily anywhere by anyone regardless of the type of industry or business conditions. It has been applied not only in Japanese companies but also in North American and European companies.
- The CEDAC System should be used as a practical technique to complete programs like TQC (Total Quality Control) and Quality Management.
- Ultimately, "management" means "enhancing quality of action." The CEDAC System triggers the actions required for effective management.
- Significant results and vitalized activities can be expected generally within six months to a year, when the CEDAC System is applied in an organization of less than one thousand people. Similar results can be obtained by larger organizations as well.

Ryuji Fukuda

CEDAC®

A Tool for Continuous
Systematic Improvement

CHAPTER 1

The Three Driving Forces for Promoting Improvement Activity

This chapter discusses how three forces work together for continual improvement.

- Developing a Reliable System
- Creating a Favorable Environment
- Practicing Together
- Actualizing the Three Driving Forces: The CEDAC System

Developing a Reliable System

Imagine a system that could reduce the number of manufacturing defects by 50% or ensure the reduction of work-in-process and production lead time. Such a system would be ideal, if it could be used successfully by anyone (not necessarily a specific person in a specific factory), anywhere and at anytime. Management techniques such as Quality Control, Production Control, and Industrial Engineering (improvements in the workplace, not only in the manufacturing plants) developed out of needs for such a system.

Such management techniques cannot be carried out by one person; only when they are implemented by a group of people are they effective. When a group works toward the completion of a project, if there is a system that everyone can depend on, everyone's actions become more efficient, and progress occurs according to plan.

Mere lecturing on the importance of increasing quality will not improve quality. A reliable system is necessary. And that will produce results only if everyone cooperates diligently and follows its steps.

Managerial Techniques That Work

- Management systems are tools.
- A useful tool must be applicable anywhere, anytime, and by anybody.
- An outstanding tool should work effectively on a company's worst problems.

A useful tool must be adaptable and easy to use. For a tool to be used to its full potential, it must be made to perfectly fit the time and place of its use. When we install a new piece of equipment or use a newly bought jig or other tool, we improve it if it does not work well in our plant. Likewise, since managerial engineering is a tool, we should be able to improve and adapt it to meet our specific needs in the best possible way.

Useful Tools

- Tools must be widely applicable.
- They must satisfactorily meet the requirements of the users.

Just as it is important to technology, so it is to managerial engineering that a company possess techniques developed on its own. The CEDAC* System introduced in this book is such an original system, and a most useful tool, created out of necessity to carry out all kinds of improvement activities.

---

* CEDAC is an acronym for the "Cause and Effect Diagram with the Addition of Cards." The original paper, "The Application of the CEDAC for Standardization and Quality Control," was awarded the 1978 Nikkei prize for a QC paper by the Deming Prize Committee in Japan. A part of that paper appears in the appendix of this book.

Over the years, CEDAC has been improved to become the final product discussed in this book. These modifications are based on practical experience. It can be used on any problem needing improvement, not necessarily those pertaining only to quality control.

Creating a Favorable Environment

Creating an environment that produces results is the second indispensable driving force of managerial engineering. Leadership and education are two of the most vital concerns related to the development of a favorable environment for continual improvement, and both are necessary to apply the CEDAC System effectively.

Leadership: Commitment of Resources for Improvements

There is a big difference between plants in which managers and supervisors provide effective leadership and those that don't. Those with strong leadership have a greater potential for improvement.

Since the CEDAC System is basically a group activity which involves the whole organization, the leadership of those in managerial positions becomes extremely important.

Furthermore, it is the higher managers who have the decisive power over the allocation of the necessary resources such as manpower, material, money, and time. Therefore, one of the crucial ways that leaders demonstrate their commitment is to allocate those resources properly to the company's improvements.

Education: Density of the Improvement Force

Another essential factor related to fostering a favorable environment is the percentage of people in the group or company who have mastered the "reliable system," the number of people who are educated about the system.

The ratio of the number of people who have mastered the reliable system to the total number of employees is the density of the improvement force. One should aim for a density of at least 10% for the best results.

If ten people are meeting to reduce defects by 50%, at least one of those ten must have the ability to lead the meeting. He or she must be able to tell the others how to use the system, designed to successfully reduce defects.

Of course, at the beginning of a project, there are many unknowns to be addressed. To avoid project members sitting around not knowing what to do, it is crucial that at least 10%, one out of every ten employees, can organize a scenario for successful improvement.

It is always important for a company to educate and train its employees. Among the so-called excellent companies, the author has not seen one that is indifferent to educational matters of this kind.

Practicing Together

The CEDAC System is a useful tool to ensure daily practice of reliable managerial engineering systems such as QC, IE, and Production Control.

For example, any golf novice will probably purchase an introductory book on golf and take lessons. However, what happens when he takes his first swing and fails miserably?

Few people would blame the book. Most people would modestly admit their own lack of practice. Then, after returning home from work, or perhaps on the weekends, they would take the time and spend part of their pocket money to practice earnestly.

In the case of management techniques, however, people often fail to read the basic instruction manuals thoroughly, or abandon them if things fail to go smoothly, even on the first try. Without sufficient practice, they might skim through several instruction manuals, one after the other, without success. In such cases, how can they ever hope to perfect their management techniques?

Skill can only be acquired when a *reliable system* is used in a *favorable environment* and *practiced constantly*. These are the key principles necessary in managerial engineering.

Lacking a suitably reliable system and shifting from system to system is like playing a game with constantly changing rules.

The success of a project depends on timing as well as the proper amount of the three driving forces for improvement, as illustrated in Figure 1. At the planning stage of a new project, we should examine our situation and foresee our chance of success by asking these three questions:

- Do we have a reliable system?
- Is the environment favorable?
- Have the members of the team concerned practiced the system enough?

If the answers are negative, what right do we have to expect success? The combined strength of the system, the environment, and the skill of the project team must outweigh the difficulty of the project. This is the key to success.

Another extremely important condition for success is the degree of worker involvement in improvement activities. We can attain greater results when everyone

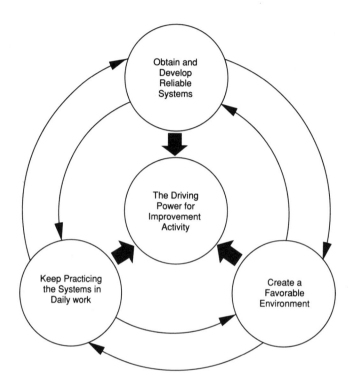

Figure 1. The Three Driving Forces

participates than when only managers and professional staff are involved in improvements. In order to facilitate worker involvement, we have devised simple and easy-to-use systems for improvement activities.

Traditionally, managers and staff have been responsible for making improvements. It was a big revolution to change the approach to involve every worker in improvement activities as well. Constant practice in daily work is the key to successful involvement of the whole workforce.

The article included as the Appendix of this book offers case studies of successful applications of the CEDAC System. Based on actual data, the article demonstrates the importance of worker involvement for success.

Each improvement the first line workers bring about may not be significant in itself. However, no matter how slight it may be, it adds a competitive advantage. Competitiveness is built on the consideration of such slight differences. What makes a company excellent in the long run is competitiveness built up by valuing every possible improvement margin.

The following story makes the point:

Two men were hiking along a mountain path when they encountered a large bear. One man quickly took off his hiking boots and put on a pair of running shoes. Watching him, the other man said, "That can't possibly save you. After all, the bear is familiar with these mountain paths, and is certainly much quicker than you." The man wearing the running shoes said, "That doesn't matter, as long as I can outrun you!"

The CEDAC system described in this textbook serves the function of the running shoes. Hopefully, this book will help you use the system more effectively and obtain excellent results.

Actualizing the Three Driving Forces: The CEDAC System

The three driving forces have been explained. But, especially for those practitioners who may feel that you know too well what "must be done" or what "should be done," the important question is how to materialize these forces.

The CEDAC system is an extremely effective tool for generating these three forces:

1. CEDAC is a reliable system which promotes improvements. It can function under different conditions in different industries and in different countries.
2. It has helped create the necessary type of favorable environments for improvement.
3. Since it is a simple method, anyone can easily acquire skill with constant practice.

Figure 2 is a summary of the CEDAC system. The upper half of Figure 2 illustrates the Seven Basic Quality Control Tools. These conventional tools arrange and integrate disorganized data into meaningful information. They are extremely effective tools in their own ways. However, in order to promote improvements, they are not sufficient.

In order to facilitate implementation and maintenance of improvements, we need to take the following actions, also shown in the lower half of Figure 2:

- Implementing countermeasures
- Confirming the results
- Standardizing
- Adhering to the standards

The CEDAC system has been created to trigger these necessary actions for improvements and consists of three processes:

- Window Analysis
- CEDAC Diagram
- Window Development

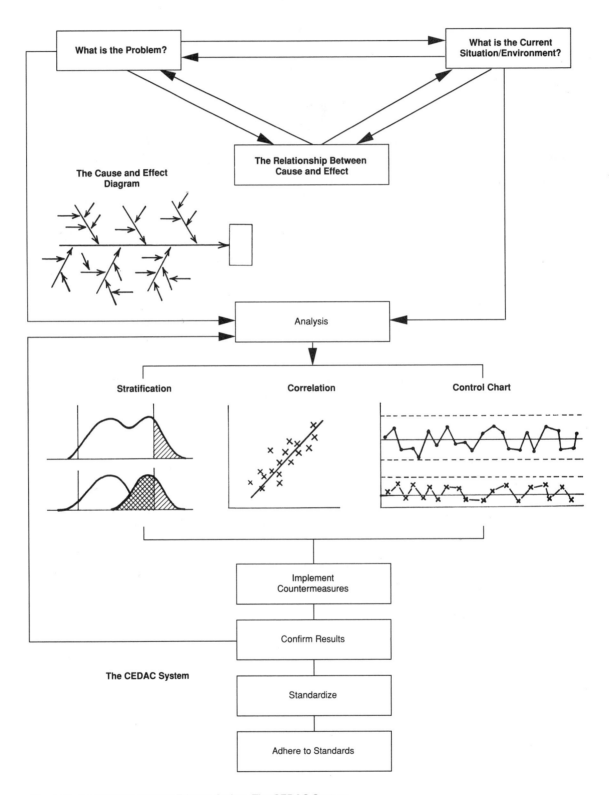

Figure 2. An Effective Tool to Trigger Action: The CEDAC System

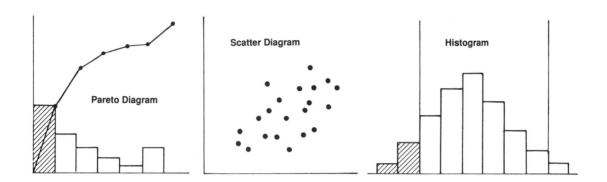

Pareto Diagram

Scatter Diagram

Histogram

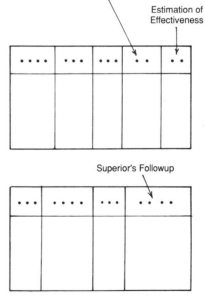

Checksheet

	10 1	2	3	4	5	6
A	///				/	
B	/	//	Ж	////	Ж	//
C			/	/		
D	//		//		/	

Window Analysis

Contents of Day-to-Day Countermeasures

Estimation of Effectiveness

Superior's Followup

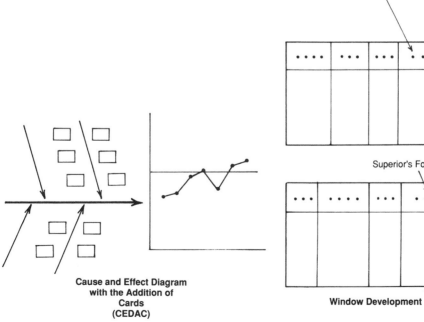

Cause and Effect Diagram with the Addition of Cards (CEDAC)

Window Development

In order to perform flawless work, we must meet two conditions:

1. The right work procedures (standards) must be established.
2. Everyone involved must understand and thoroughly practice these procedures.

The CEDAC system is a technique to achieve the above conditions with many people's involvement. In order to carry out the ordinary on a large scale, we must have a systematic approach. The next three chapters discuss each of the processes of the CEDAC System in depth.

CHAPTER 2

Window Analysis:
Accurate Fact-Finding For
Preventive Countermeasures

This chapter discusses Window Analysis, the first element of the CEDAC system. There are five parts to the discussion:

- Window Analysis
- Ways to Eliminate Defects
- Window Analysis Exercise: Six Case Studies
- Analyzing the Results of the Window
- Directions for Countermeasures

Window Analysis

This method analyzes concrete facts about the various defective outcomes which occur in daily work and attempts to categorize them from a management perspective. Using this technique creates habits for gathering facts correctly, categorizing data for measurement, and establishing effective countermeasures.

Figure 3 shows the basic structure of the Window. Party X and Party Y are people or functional groups who interact with each other to carry out work on a day-to-day basis.

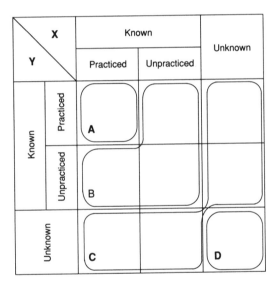

Figure 3. Basic Structure of the Window

When a problem is broad and cross-functional, Party X and Party Y may represent two different departments. As a rule, Party X is chosen to indicate "one's own side." Table 1 shows some examples of such horizontal combinations of Party X and Party Y.

X	Current Process	Design Department	Manufacturing Department	Our Company
Y	Previous Process	Manufacturing Department	Sales	Customer

Table 1.

On the other hand, when a problem is confined to one functional group, Party X and Party Y represent two parties within one group. As a rule, Party X is used to indicate the "higher rank" in the organization. Table 2 shows some examples of such vertical combinations.

X	Group Leader	Supervisor	Section Chief	Department Manager
Y	Members	Members	Group Leaders	Section Chief

Table 2 .

In any case, it is important to select a proper combination of Party X and Party Y that can take concrete action against the problem.

Definition of Words

Known: The right procedures to prevent defects are established and communicated to all concerned.

Unknown: The right procedures to prevent defects are not established yet.

Practiced: The procedures are practiced 100% of the time.

Unpracticed: The procedures are not practiced all of the time (Ranges from zero to almost 100 percent).

With the above definitions, we have four categories as follows:

Category A

The right procedures to prevent defects are established and both parties know and correctly practice these procedures. This is the ideal situation.

Category B

The right procedures to prevent defects are established and there is someone who does not practice them correctly. This is an adherence problem. There are three subcategories:

- *Situation 1*: Although the correct method is known, there are careless mistakes resulting in non-adherence to procedure.
- *Situation 2*: Although the correct method is known, someone lacks the skills and cannot utilize the knowledge. Therefore, the procedure is not adhered to properly.

• *Situation 3*: Although the correct method is known, lack of time, manpower and/or money leads to abbreviation of the procedure.

Category C

The right procedures to prevent defects are established but one of the two parties, who should have been informed, does not know the procedure. This is a communication problem. Many defective work outcomes develop in this manner.

Category D

There is no correct standard procedure for eliminating defects. Since the technical problems causing defects remain unsolved, neither party knows how to eliminate those problems. In office work situations, defects caused by lack of effective rules fall into this category. This is a standardization problem.

Joharry's Window

Getting a hint from the basic structure of Joharry's Window (Figure 4), Window Analysis has been developed to its present form. In deference to the origin, let us introduce it here.

Joharry's Window was devised by Joseph Luft and Harry Ingram to describe communication between two parties.

Category I refers to what both you and I know. Category IV refers to that which neither party knows. Categories II and III refer to that which is only known to one of the two parties.

Obviously, in the practical situation, "knowing" and "doing" are two separate issues. Thus, to improve the function of the window as a tool to analyze problems, the new window subdivides the "known" category into "known-practiced" and "known-unpracticed."

I You	Know	Don't Know
Know	I	II
Don't Know	III	IV

Figure 4. Joharry's Window

Ways to Eliminate Defects

To eliminate all defective outcomes of work, all situations described by the Window Analysis Categories B, C, and D must be changed to Category A. (see Figure 3). In other words, defects are eliminated when you establish the effective standards for operational and technical procedure, you educate all concerned, and you practice the standards rigorously.

Systematic Improvement Occurs Progressively

Two examples follow:

1. Category C → Category B → Category A
   Everyone should be informed of the correct methods and technical standards for eliminating defects. Everyone should adhere to the standards.
2. Category D → Category C → Category B → Category A
   If the current procedure or technical standards are inadequate, they should be revised seeking a technically better method or a way to reduce costs. Everyone must be informed of the new procedure, and it should be executed correctly.

Window Analysis Exercise: Six Case Studies

All defective outcomes that emerge in the workplace should fall into one of the sections in Figure 5, except Address 1. Since Address 1 is Category A, the ideal condition, there are no defects that need to be eliminated in this category.

In order to practice methods of classification with the Window, let us use six simple case studies. In each case study the facts of the situation are presented followed by an analysis using the Window. Since these cases are designed for the purpose of the Window Analysis exercise, the descriptions include a range of possible answers. However, it should be remembered that in reality there will be just one best way to understand the situation. If you dig into the root causes deeply enough, you should always be able to identify the most accurate address for a given problem.

Studying these six cases will help clarify the method of classification. Try to use it on problems or defects that you currently face. It can be used on a wide range of problems, not only quality problems.

Analyze and calculate the number of cases which fall into the three categories. By understanding which category has the most defects, your main weakness can be identified from a management perspective. Then, you can improve the weakness and prevent future recurrence of similar problems.

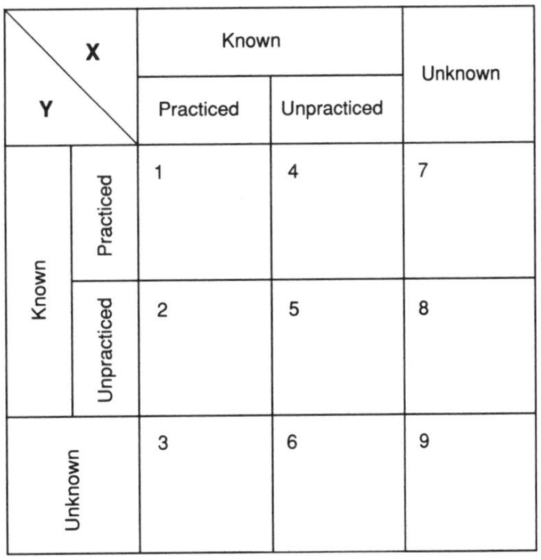

X / Y	Known		Unknown
	Practiced	Unpracticed	
Known Practiced	1	4	7
Known Unpracticed	2	5	8
Unknown	3	6	9

Figure 5. The Nine Window Frames

Case 1: The Coffee That No One Drank

Situation

Three seminars were held simultaneously at a hotel. It had been prearranged that a table with coffee and doughnuts would be available in the lobby during the two twenty-minute breaks at 10 a.m. and 3 p.m..

However, the organizer forgot to inform one of the lecturers, Speaker F, about the break schedule. Consequently, Speaker F's class took breaks at other than the scheduled times and did not receive the refreshments as planned.

Window Analysis

    X: Speaker F

    Y: Organizer

The time for the coffee breaks had been prearranged. However, due to carelessness, the organizer failed to inform Speaker F. Thus, the organizer falls into the "known-unpracticed" category in the Window, Address 5.

On the other hand, Speaker F, who should have been informed of the arranged coffee break times, falls into the "unknown" category. This analysis leads us to Address 8.

However, if Speaker F had chosen to reflect upon the situation, he would not be able to place simple blame saying, "The organizer did not tell me." Since the fact that the seminars had two breaks was common knowledge, he should have notified the organizer immediately upon noticing the oversight.

If Speaker F is sincere and admits his fault of not inquiring about the coffee breaks, his part is also interpreted as "unpracticed." In this analysis, the same problem falls into Address 5.

Thus the case could fall in either Address 5 or 8. Both sides decided that following up on Address 5 would lead to more effective and thorough action.

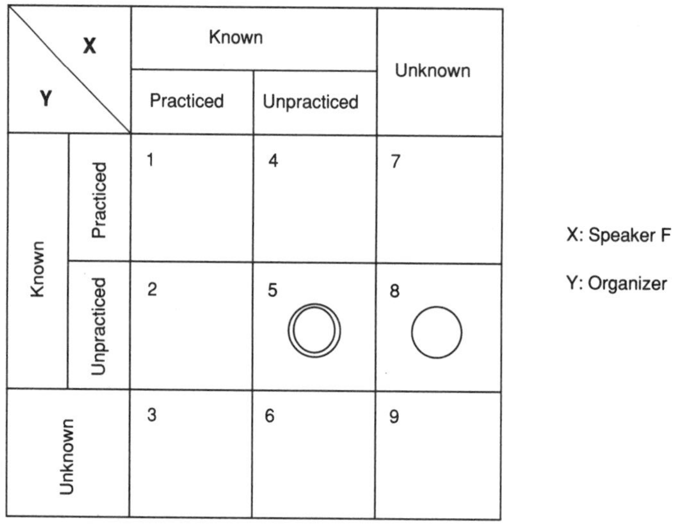

X \ Y		Known		Unknown
		Practiced	Unpracticed	
Known	Practiced	1	4	7
Known	Unpracticed	2	5 ◎	8 ○
Known	Unknown	3	6	9

X: Speaker F

Y: Organizer

Figure 6. Case 1

Case 2: A Motor Failure

Situation

After one week of use at the customer's site, a continuous-duty motor broke. The motor failure was caused by a melted power lead wire.

At the design stage of the motor, an electrical engineer and a mechanical engineer worked together. The electrical engineer knew that a larger size power lead wire must be used for such a continuous-duty motor. Assuming that the mechanical engineer was also aware of this fact, the electrical engineer did not refer to it in the remarks column of the specifications. When writing new specifications, a designer was supposed to fill in such information.

The mechanical engineer knew the relationship between the size of wire to be used and the purpose of the motor. However, when he actually designed the motor, he failed to include information about the wire size because he did not have the skill to use this information on the drawing.

According to the plan, a regular size power lead wire was installed.

Window Analysis

The electrical engineer, assuming that the mechanical engineer would know that the lead wire had to be larger, failed to write this in the remarks column. Thus, he fell into the category, "known-unpracticed."

The mechanical engineer had the correct knowledge, but lacked the skill to communicate that knowledge properly. Therefore, he fell into the category "known-unpracticed." This accident falls into Address 5 of Figure 7.

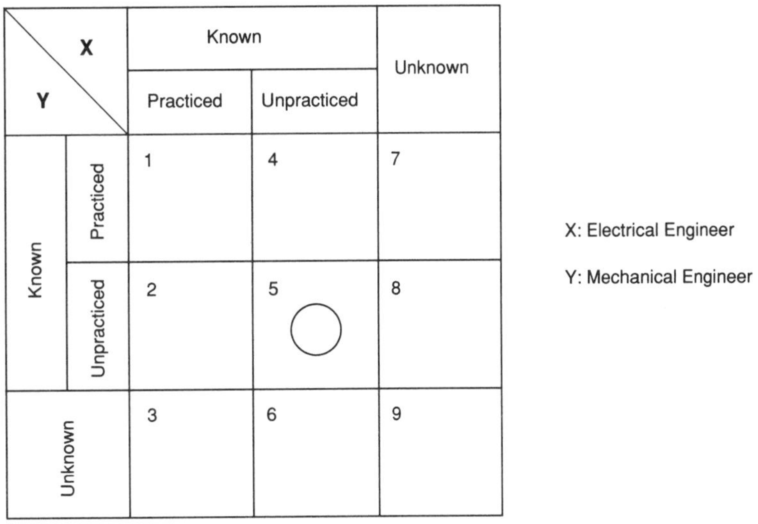

Y \ X		Known		Unknown
		Practiced	Unpracticed	
Known	Practiced	1	4	7
	Unpracticed	2	5 ◯	8
Unknown		3	6	9

X: Electrical Engineer

Y: Mechanical Engineer

Figure 7. Case 2

Case 3: The Delayed Delivery

Situation

During the assembly process of Product A, an assembly worker detected some defective parts mixed in a container supplied by the previous drilling process. The defective parts had holes in the wrong place. Due to these defects, the assemblers were three units short and could not complete the order of 200 units scheduled for the day.

The assemblers notified the drillers of the problem, nonetheless it took an extra day for drilling to make substitute parts and send them to assembly. It also upset the schedule of the subsequent process of reliability testing and inspection. Since the delivery date of Product A was drawing extremely close, the delay was critical. As a result, the company failed to meet the requested delivery date and lost potential business opportunities with the customer.

Soon after the incident, the facts were investigated. The drilling machine was equipped with a fool-proof device to prevent holes from being drilled at the wrong place. On that particular day, however, the device was not working, so the drilling operator temporarily detached it, continued working, and produced several defective parts by mistake.

Window Analysis
    X: *Assembly Process*
    Y: *Drilling Process*

The assembly process was conducted correctly, and therefore X is designated as "known-practiced." The drilling process was supposed to operate the machine with the fool-proof device, but the device was detached. Therefore Y is "known-unpracticed." This gives us Address 2, indicated in Figure 8.

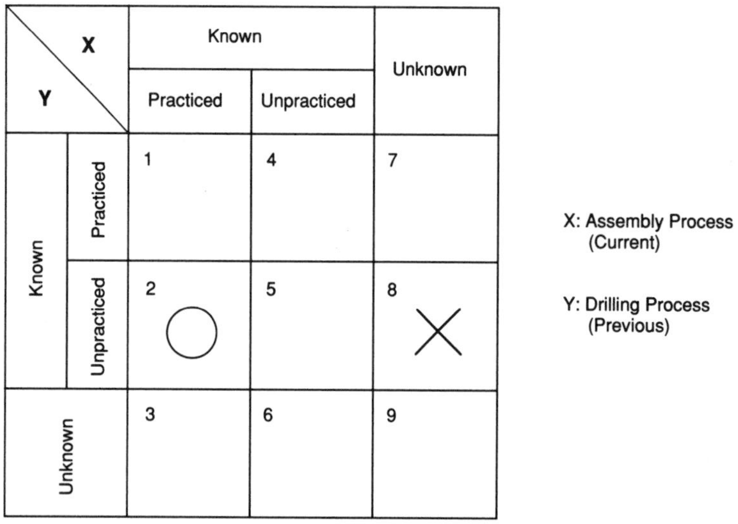

Figure 8. Case 3 (#1)

A frequent mistake in plotting this case on the Window is to mark it as Address 8 by considering that the assembly process did not know the previous process was operating without the fool-proof device. However, Category C (Unknown) indicates situations where some individuals do not know what they are supposed to know. In this case, the responsibility to take a countermeasure lies with the drilling process, not the assembly process.

If we consider the case as in Figure 9, where X is the drilling process supervisor and Y is a drilling process worker, then Party Y, who detached the fool-proof device despite the rule that he must operate the machine with the device on, falls into the category "known-unpracticed."

For the supervisor, Party X, there are two interpretations:

1. It is the responsibility of the supervisor to check the work of his workers, regardless of the reason. Therefore, he falls into "known-unpracticed." This gives us Address 5.

2. Since the supervisor knew the indispensable nature of the fool-proof device and gave enough guidance to his people, it was beyond his imagination that any worker would continue the drilling process without it. In other words, if the supervisor thought that nothing more could be done on his part, he would fall into the category "known-practiced," Address 2.

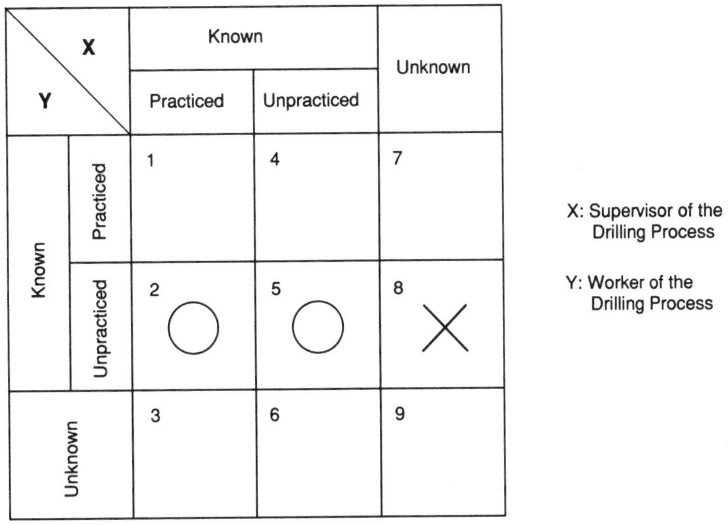

X Y	Known		Unknown
	Practiced	Unpracticed	
Known / Practiced	1	4	7
Known / Unpracticed	2 ◯	5 ◯	8 ✕
Unknown	3	6	9

X: Supervisor of the Drilling Process

Y: Worker of the Drilling Process

Figure 9. Case 3 (#2)

This case cannot fall into Address 8, because that would indicate a situation where the supervisor does not know what he is supposed to know. It is unthinkable that the supervisor did not know the existing rule that, in order to avoid careless mistakes, the machine must be operated with the fool-proof device.

As shown in the above examples, the "practiced" of the supervisor refers to the education and guidance he provides his workers. This helps them eliminate defects and learn correct methods. Therefore, the key question in this case is how well the supervisor fulfilled his responsibility to coach and check his people's work.

Case 4: A Slip of the Mind

Situation

A 6-person design group and the manufacturing section chief had a meeting to discuss the specifications of a special made-to-order product.

The designer in charge forgot to include on the drawing a special specification item discussed at the meeting.

On the manufacturing side, although the section chief knew of the details of the specifications, he forgot to tell the group leader in charge of production. Therefore, the group leader, despite the fact that he followed the drawing properly, ended up with a defective product.

Since the product was quite large, its rework required much time and money, and a considerable loss was incurred.

Window Analysis

As far as combinations of Party X and Party Y go, we can consider Figures 10, 11, and 12. However, in terms of corrective action, Figure 12 would definitely be the most effective.

Since the designer forgot to include the details of the meeting on the drawing, he falls into the category "known-unpracticed."

The section chief failed to inform the group leader of the details of the meeting, so he, too, falls into the category "known-unpracticed."

Since both the designer and the section chief were "known-unpracticed," this problem falls into Address 5 (Figure 12).

The group leader in charge of production lacked the information that should have been on the blueprint (Figure 10) as well as the information from his section chief (Figure 11). He falls into the category "unknown" in both instances, and the Window Address is 6, or Category C. After all, he did not have the necessary information.

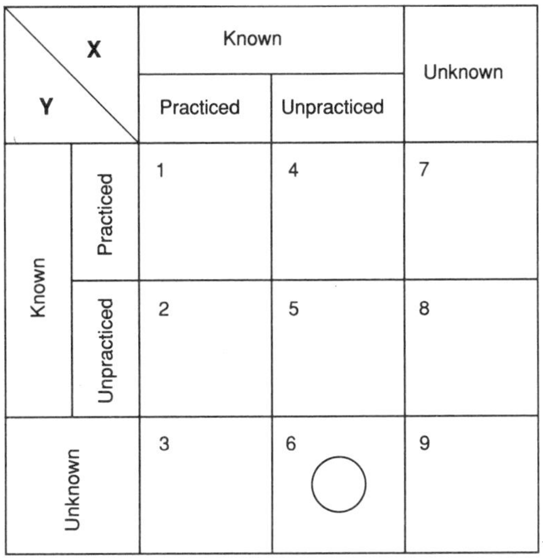

X \ Y		Known		Unknown
		Practiced	Unpracticed	
Known	Practiced	1	4	7
	Unpracticed	2	5	8
Unknown		3	6 ◯	9

X: Designer

Y: Group Leader

Figure 10. Case 4 (#1)

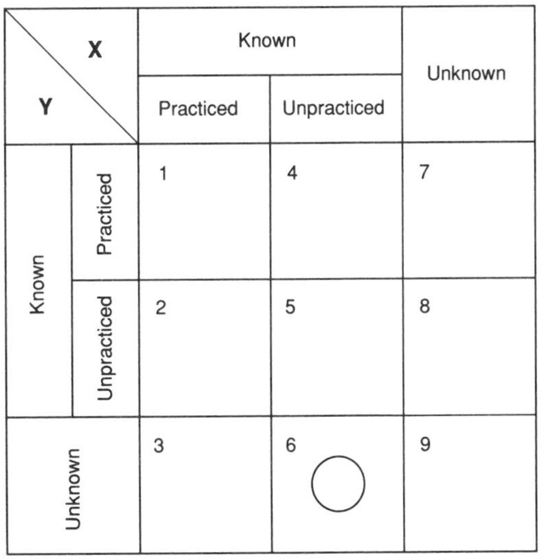

X \ Y		Known		Unknown
		Practiced	Unpracticed	
Known	Practiced	1	4	7
	Unpracticed	2	5	8
Unknown		3	6 ◯	9

X: ManufacturingSection Chief

Y: Group Leader

Figure 11. Case 4 (#2)

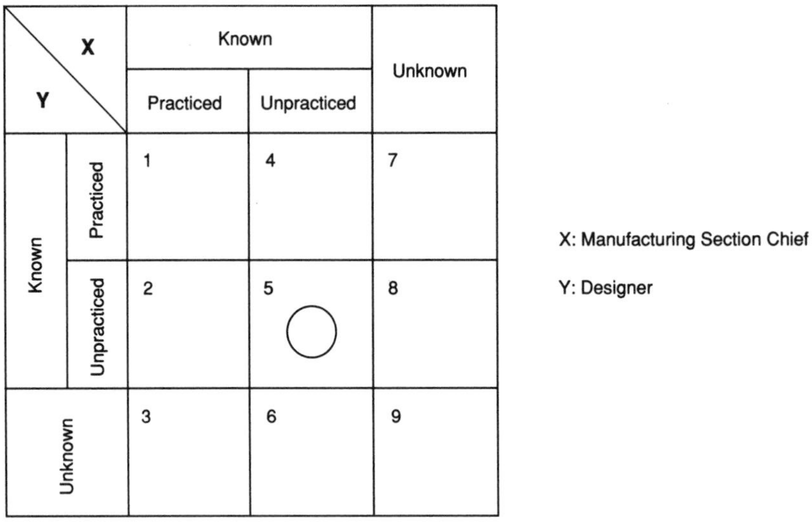

X \ Y	Known		Unknown
	Practiced	Unpracticed	
Known — Practiced	1	4	7
Known — Unpracticed	2	5 ◯	8
Unknown	3	6	9

X: Manufacturing Section Chief

Y: Designer

Figure 12. Case 4 (#3)

Case 5: The Ten-day Wait

Situation

An engine generator for civil engineering use was shipped from the manufacturer to a customer. In order to avoid possible damages due to vibration during transportation, the manufacturer placed a vibration-proof rubber sheet between the main body of the generator and the bed. The attached instruction manual included the information that the rubber sheet must be removed and the main body must be firmly fixed on the bed before the generator is installed and used at the site.

The construction people at the customer's site, feeling accustomed to such generators, didn't read the instruction manual. Without knowing what would happen, they started running the machine with the rubber sheet still on it. Immediately, the lead wire broke in several places and the generator became useless. Since the construction site was in a remote mountain area, it took ten days for a substitute generator to arrive. Consequently, construction was much delayed.

Window Analysis

X: *Manufacturer*

Y: *Customer*

The manufacturer provided an instruction manual which clearly stated that the generator should be used only after removal of the rubber sheet. Therefore, he falls into the category "known-practiced."

On the other hand, the customer's construction workers did not know what would happen if the generator was used while the rubber sheet was still attached. Thus they fall into "unknown," giving us Address 3.

However, the accident could have been averted if the construction workers had read the instruction manual. They knew they should have read it ("known-unpracticed"). Thus, this case could also be interpreted as falling into Address 2.

In an actual case, we should choose which is more appropriate based on the facts and consider how to prevent the same problem from happening again. For example, Address 3 indicates the best solution would be to educate the concerned people that whenever a new engine generator comes, they should check the rubber sheet and remove it. Address 2 indicates the best solution would be to convince people that they must practice reading an instruction manual every time they receive a new machine.

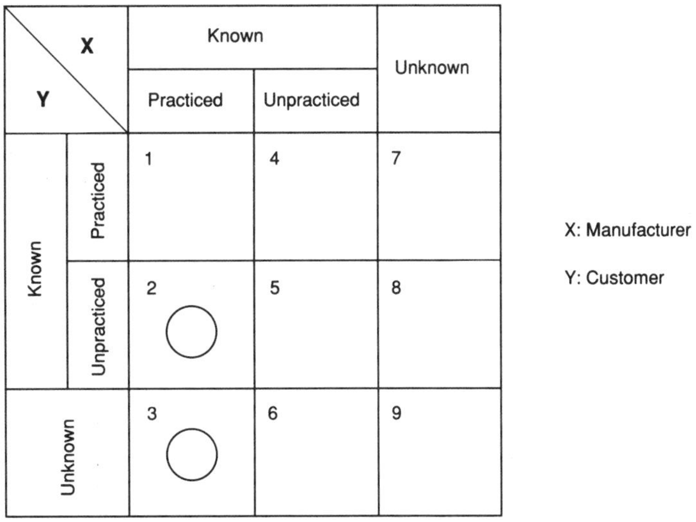

Y \ X		Known		Unknown
		Practiced	Unpracticed	
Known	Practiced	1	4	7
Known	Unpracticed	2 ◯	5	8
Unknown		3 ◯	6	9

X: Manufacturer

Y: Customer

Figure 13. Case 5

Case 6: An Accident Six Years Later

Situation

An equipment manufacturer designed and manufactured a large cable stranding machine. Both the design department and manufacturing department were completely familiar with the necessary technology and expertise. Thinking that the required quality had been built-in during the production process, they sent the product to the customer.

Six years later, the shaft snapped, and the customer filed a claim for damages. Investigations proved that the cause of the breakdown was metal fatigue.

The customer was also using similar equipment produced by a rival company of the equipment manufacturer. This equipment had been operating correctly for the past eight years.

Window Analysis

Six years later, a claim was filed against a product which both the design and manufacturing departments had considered to be Category A (Address 1) merchandise. The defective product was examined. Compared to that of the rival company, it was inferior in the quality and hardness of the shaft material, as well as in the method of shaft fitting.

At the time the equipment was being manufactured, neither department knew of the weaknesses. Therefore this problem should fall into Address 9 or Category D. Thus, what was thought to be Category A, fell into Category D.

To maintain Category A status, reliability engineering is necessary. This discipline sets the required quality of products as compared to that of one's competitors in terms of designing and manufacturing and determines how to build that quality into products during the production process.

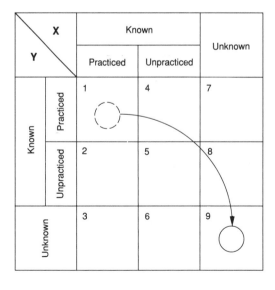

Figure 14. Case 6

Analyzing the Results of the Window

Table 3 shows the results of Window Analysis at five different companies. The data on defective work outcomes were collected for a certain period of time, classified into Categories B, C, or D, and expressed in percentages.

It is noteworthy that, in general, Categories B and C have higher numbers than Category D.

The percentage in each category naturally depends on the type of industry and the business conditions. Furthermore, even in the same company, depending on the department and product line, the ratio may vary.

There is no such thing as an optimum ratio of categories. What is important is to know one's own situation by classifying the actual problems into categories and finding out the relative seriousness of each category — B, C, and D.

Of equal importance is whether the necessary manpower and capital have been mobilized to deal with the problems in Categories B, C, and D, depending on their nature and frequency of occurrence.

The examples are based on the number of defective outcomes, but results can also be analyzed according to total monetary loss incurred due to defects.

Window Analysis is based on a simple concept: an effective countermeasure cannot be designed without grasping the facts accurately.

One major advantage of Window Analysis lies in that it cannot be used unless the details causing the problem have been clearly identified.

In other words, the goal is not to simply plot the problem on the Window when a defect occurs. It must serve as a trigger for action, forcing those involved to immediately search for the facts. This is the greatest strength of Window Analysis. In essence, it helps build a corporation's strength by initiating actions that fortify and improve it.

Another advantage is the fact that the results of Window Analysis approach the problem from the perspective of management. They encourage preventive measures which focus directly upon the overall organizational weaknesses. Thus, it is different from "fire-fighting" in which each problem is dealt with one by one as it shows up. While you are busy fixing a problem, a similar one pops up in another area. It goes on and on, and you have to keep chasing problems. Window Analysis puts an end to that.

Moreover, the Window should not be used to blame the responsible parties by analyzing defective outcomes. It is essential to foster an attitude and atmosphere which encourages the people involved to be constructive in making preventive measures.

	Company S (cable, wire)	Company M (heavy electric)	Company Y (auto)	Company T (semi-conductors)	Company F (steel)
B	50	45	50	35	50
C	40	30	35	30	45
D	10	25	15	35	5
Total %	100	100	100	100	100

Table 3. Classification of the Causes of Quality Defects According to the Window

The special characteristics of Window Analysis, as described thus far, can be summarized in two points:

1. Window Analysis effectively triggers action to uncover the cause of any given problem. Without finding true causes, effective prevention cannot occur.
2. By totaling the results of Window Analysis, weaknesses from a management perspective fall into three categories:
   • weak adherence to standards
   • lack of communication and education about the standards
   • inability to establish the standard

Knowing the true source of the problem, we can become effective in preventing defects.

Directions for Countermeasures

As shown in Figure 15, proper countermeasures should be chosen according to the results of Window Analysis.

If your weakness is Category D (the right procedures are not established), move on to the CEDAC Diagram introduced in the following chapter.

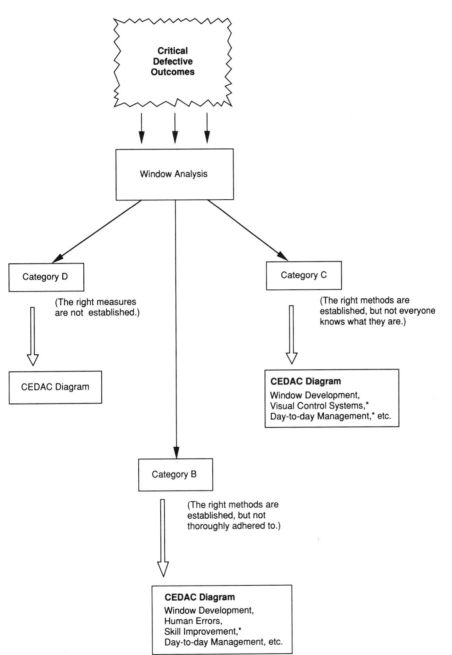

Figure 15. Countermeasures for Window Analysis

If Category B (the right methods are established but not practiced rigorously), do the Window Development (introduced in Chapter IV), The CEDAC diagram, Human Errors, Skill Improvement, etc.

If Category C (the right methods are established but not communicated to all concerned), work on Window Development, a CEDAC diagram, Visual Control Systems, Day-to-Day Management, etc.

It should be noted that if you incorporate these countermeasures into your system based on the Window Analysis results, you will actually be improving organizational effectiveness for prevention.

Among such countermeasures, this book elaborates on the CEDAC Diagram and Window Development.

CHAPTER 3

Establishing Standards
(Right Methods)
for Everyone to Use

If Window Analysis indicates weakness in Category D, and the right procedures are not established, then the CEDAC diagram will be most useful. This chapter includes:

- Synopsis and Special Features of The CEDAC Diagram
- How to Make and Use a CEDAC Diagram

Synopsis and Special Features of The CEDAC Diagram

The CEDAC Diagram was created to deal with Category D problems, namely situations in which a reliable method has not been established. A standard is set by integrating the knowledge and experience of everyone involved: workers, engineers, supervisors, and management.

The term "standard" refers to a reliable method or procedure which prevents the occurrence of defective outcomes. Whether or not these standards are officially written on paper is irrelevant.

If the current standards allowing defects or problems to arise are not changed, the process will continue to produce defects. The CEDAC Diagram was developed in the quest for an effective system to establish reliable standards that eliminate serious defects caused by lack of such a reliable method. Work that needs a dependable standard, regardless of the task, needs better methods.

Even standards that seem to meet the requirements at the present time, can often be replaced by better (more stable, less expensive) methods.

The CEDAC Diagram was created out of the necessity to set such living standards.

Steps 1 to 7 in Figure 16 are the components of the CEDAC Diagram. The shape of the CEDAC Diagram resembles that of the Cause-and-Effect Diagram, but its goal is completely different.

First, let us summarize the Effect Side of the CEDAC Diagram.

Steps 1-3 on the Effect Side of the CEDAC Diagram

The Effect Side of the CEDAC Diagram consists of three steps, shown in Figure 16.

Step 1: What needs to be improved? How should the results be measured?
Step 2: What is the time interval for data collection?
Step 3: What is the target for improvement? Upon achieving the target, how much profit can be expected?

These final decisions must be made by the leader of the improvement team. Of course, it is valuable to exchange opinions with people involved in the project, but final decisions must be made by the person in charge. Otherwise, when urgent and serious matters have to be dealt with promptly, the decision-making process tends to be ambiguous.

When a broad problem involves other sections and divisions, it is necessary to organize a project-oriented team. An organization which utilizes the CEDAC

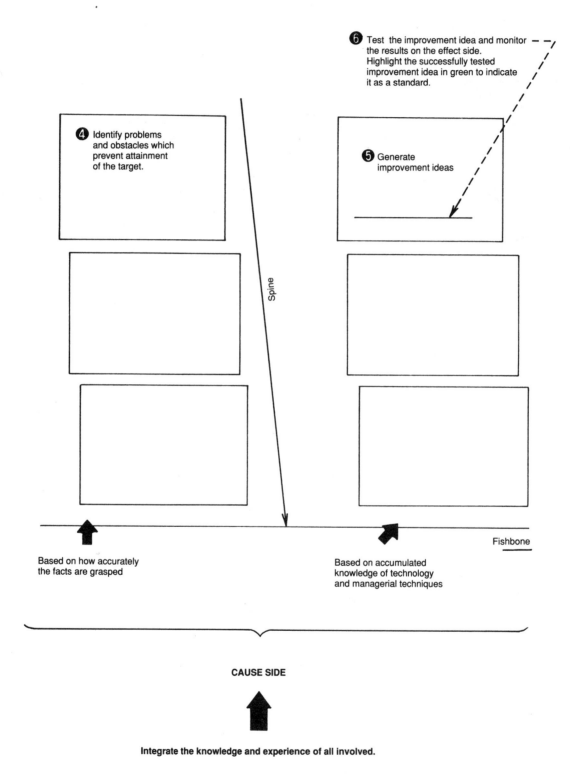

6 Test the improvement idea and monitor the results on the effect side. Highlight the successfully tested improvement idea in green to indicate it as a standard.

4 Identify problems and obstacles which prevent attainment of the target.

Spine

5 Generate improvement ideas

Fishbone

Based on how accurately the facts are grasped

Based on accumulated knowledge of technology and managerial techniques

CAUSE SIDE

Integrate the knowledge and experience of all involved.

Figure 16. The Seven Essentials of the CEDAC Diagram

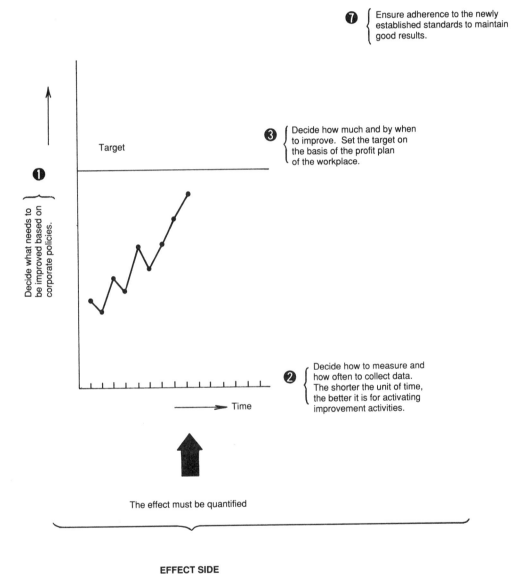

❼ { Ensure adherence to the newly established standards to maintain good results.

Target

❶

Decide what needs to be improved based on corporate policies.

❸ { Decide how much and by when to improve. Set the target on the basis of the profit plan of the workplace.

❷ { Decide how to measure and how often to collect data. The shorter the unit of time, the better it is for activating improvement activities.

→ Time

The effect must be quantified

EFFECT SIDE

The leader is the final decision-maker.

Diagram must be a team comprised of the management and engineers who are involved in the matter as well as the supervisors and workers.

Who should be the leader? How many people should be involved? Such factors depend on the size of the project and its purpose.

In any case, the Effect Side must be determined by the leaders. Targets for improvement must be closely connected to the profit plan of the workplace, as well as that of the company.

There are often cases in which there is no clear-cut understanding of what to improve, or one cannot decide how to measure the improvement results. In such cases, improvement, as well as standardization of the improvement results, become impossible. It is crucial that both the conditions to be improved and the method of measurement are explicit.

Table 4 illustrates suitable types of improvement objects for the Effect Side of the CEDAC Diagram.

The knowledge and experience of all those involved can be combined effectively to make improvements. For reasons given later in the explanation of the Cause Side, the Effect Side must be quantified. If the numerical data are not readily available, you must devise a way to quantify the improvement objective including using a relative ratio.

Steps 4-6 on the Cause Side of the CEDAC Diagram

Next we shall elaborate on the Cause Side of Figure 16.

One feature of the Cause Side is the fact that it guarantees equal participation of all people involved. This is described in *Steps 4, 5,* and *6.*

In *Step 4,* the obstacles that hinder attainment of the goal are written on cards. These are called "fact cards" and are attached to the CEDAC Diagram.

Everyone participates in the card-writing process from their own strengths. For example, managers and supervisors might rely on their past experiences. Engineers might draw on their specialized knowledge. Workers are the closest to the source. Everyone must tap their own resources.

The fact cards are given to the leader in charge of managing the CEDAC Diagram activity. These cards are categorized and attached to the left side of the spines in Figure 16.

Depending on the nature of the problem, at this point, the Seven Basic QC Tools (Figure 2) can be applied to interpret the quantitative data and utilize the information obtained.

If the data are not quantified, it is effective to use the New Seven QC Tools such as the Affinity Diagram and Relations Diagram (see appendix).

What is to be improved?	• Measurement (Devise a way to quantify results.)
Quality defect reduction	• Fraction of defects • Failure cost (Monetary loss due to defects divided by total cost.) • Number of defects • Number of claims
Work-in-process reduction	• Amount of work-in-process • Number or rate of failure to meet delivery date • Production lead time • Average inventory level (Inventory level at the beginning of the term and inventory level at the end of the term divided by 2.) • Inventory turnover (Annual sales amount divided by average inventory level.)
Productivity improvement	• Labor productivity • Set-up time reduction ratio • Ratio of workers with multiple skills • Machine productivity • MTBF (Mean Time Between Failures) • Frequency of equipment failure • Rate of robotization • Equipment utilization ratio • Overall equipment effectiveness (Availability $\times$ Performance efficiency $\times$ Rate of quality products.)
Engineering and administrative work improvement	• Rate of new products in product mix • Profitability of new products • Number or rate of computer input errors • Achievement level of Visual Control Systems • Conformity between budget and actual result • Efficiency of visiting customers • Accomplishment of goals for attaining new orders • Number and contents of claims • Effectiveness of design reviews

Table 4. Objects of Improvements (Example)

In *Step 5*, everyone participating in the project submits their ideas for improvement. The leader or his assistant attaches the cards. These cards are now called "improvement cards."

In this process, too, the leader sorts out the cards. All the cards, however, are always displayed. The leader should not choose cards on the basis of his own judgment or preference.

The displayed cards, by common consent, fall into the following categories: Unusable, Of Interest, Under Preparation, and Under Test. "Under Test" refers to a trial test run of an improvement idea. While implementing the idea, the results are carefully monitored to find out whether there is any change on the Effect Side.

The test results determine the success of the idea. Therefore, the Effect Side must be quantified.

Let's say two improvement ideas on one obstacle are submitted: one by a worker and one by a manager. The idea with the better test results definitely wins in the end. Thus the Cause Side guarantees equal participation by all those involved. Whereas, when improvement ideas are simply discussed in a meeting, ideas submitted by managers would probably be used more frequently.

These are the distinctive features of the CEDAC Diagram:

• The Effect Side follows the direction of an organization's policies.
• The Cause Side allows everyone's autonomous participation.

In *Step 6*, the idea for improvement is put into practice. Those that are successful on the Effect Side are underlined in green highlighter. This becomes the standard. The card is now called the "standard card."

In many cases where the CEDAC Diagram fails to help achieve a target effect, the following problem is common: Workers submit improvement cards in steps 4 and 5 and don't submit any cards thereafter. In addition, of the cards they do submit, usually none reveal anything that wasn't known before the CEDAC project started.

In such situations, a CEDAC leader must encourage participants to look more carefully at the facts or to unearth the real problem. Or if the improvement cards are weak, then he should lead them to polish their own knowledge or to develop their own solutions.

If use of the CEDAC Diagram stops here, it will serve as nothing more than a means of organizing thoughts. It is not a magic wand by which everything can be solved without effort, simply jotting things down. As with Window Analysis, the beauty of the CEDAC Diagram lies in its ability to trigger the necessary action for improvement.

Step 7: Adhering to the Standards to Maintain Good Results

Step 7 is the stage to adhere to the set standards and maintain good results.

By setting standards, the CEDAC Diagram is a practical procedure to deal with Category D. However, the whole card writing process can obviously be used effectively on Category C (so that everyone is well informed) as well as Category B (adhering to standards).

How to Make and Use a CEDAC Diagram

The explanation of how to make a CEDAC Diagram and the important points to remember follow. In practice, feel free to create your own application, but do not skip over the items or change them arbitrarily.

Draw the Diagram

The CEDAC Diagram should be drawn on a white piece of paper, approximately 2 meters by 1 meter. Draw the Effect Side on the right, and draw the Cause Side on the left.

Define the Focus

The focus for improvement should be the one which contributes the most to the profit target of the workplace. For example, choosing the improvement focus on the basis of Pareto analysis works well.

Choose the Project Leader

Each CEDAC Diagram must have its own project leader. The CEDAC leader should be the actual person in charge of the improvement project.

The CEDAC project leader promotes activity at all stages of the CEDAC project. The leader must exert leadership skill that will pull together all those involved to complete the CEDAC project.

Write the name of the project leader and the starting date on the lower right corner of the CEDAC Diagram.

Measure Results

Devise a way to measure the results on the Effect Side. Depending upon the improvement subject, the measure devised may be other than those mentioned in Table 4. One must be especially creative when striving to improve productivity and work quality in the engineering and administrative sectors. How to measure improvement is extremely important. Therefore, do not spare time, effort, or cost on these discussions and necessary preparations.

It is important to measure and plot the results over the shortest time interval possible (e.g. every hour, every day, every week, or every other week). This is necessary in order to understand the relationship between the test of the improvement idea and its results as soon as possible. The shorter the time interval, the sooner the improvement will be activated. The Day-to-Day Management System is very effective for this purpose.

Set the Target

The project leader sets the target. He makes sure all involved understand the details of the target and the target date.

One thing must be made clear: how the attainment of the target will contribute to the profit targets of the workplace and the company. This should be demonstrated in concrete terms. For example: "There is currently a loss of X dollars per month. That will be reduced to a loss of Y dollars per month," or "Attaining the target will enhance the competitiveness of the whole corporation. The numbers of orders received will increase, creating an increase in profits of X dollars per month." It is good to express the advantage in monetary terms. After all, money is easy to understand. It is a universal measure all over the world.

Format the Effect Side

Decide on the format of the Effect Side. Draw it in. The CEDAC Effect Side must consist of a visual display of the quantified improvement results and target. The Effect Side is illustrated by means of line and bar graphs, control charts, etc. (Refer to Figure 17.)

Gather the "Fact Cards"

Attach the fact cards to the left of the spines on the Cause Side. (Refer to Figure 18.)

The problems and obstacles needing to be solved for the attainment of the improvement target must be written on the cards. Although concise, they must cover the necessary details adequately.

The person submitting the card must put his initials in the bottom left corner of the card. This is so that everyone knows to whom to go for further details. These cards are written by everyone involved in the project (e.g. managers, engineers, supervisors, and workers) in response to the leader's call for action.

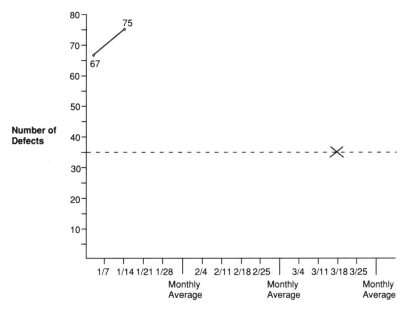

Focus: Reduction of Stamping Defects
Measurement: Number of Defects/Week

Target: Reducing the number of defects by 50% (35 defects/week)
Leader: Ryuji Fukuda
Starting Date: January 14, 1986
Target Date: March 18, 1986

Figure 17. The Effect Side of the CEDAC Diagram

The extent to which the facts have been grasped correctly plays a large role in the quality of the "fact cards." Simply glancing at the raw data is not sufficient. For example, choose the main problem by using Pareto, or analyze the current distribution by using a histogram. Or discover significant abnormalities by utilizing a control chart. These are useful and effective techniques.

In order to integrate unquantifiable data (so-called language data) in an organized manner, use the New Seven QC Tools. Figure 19 is an example of organizing the Total Productive Maintenance (TPM) problems using one of these new tools, the Affinity Diagram.

The fact cards are categorized by content and placed on the left side of the spines by the leader. The cards may describe the observation of problems and obstacles. In other cases, when the above-mentioned tools are applied, they may state the processed information.

If the contents of two or more cards are the same, they should be synthesized to one card, or attached to the chart together. (Refer to Figure 18.)

It is best to categorize the spines according to the contents of the fact cards. If you set the categories in advance (for instance, by the 5Ms: management, manpower, machinery, material, and method), it will place limits on thinking.

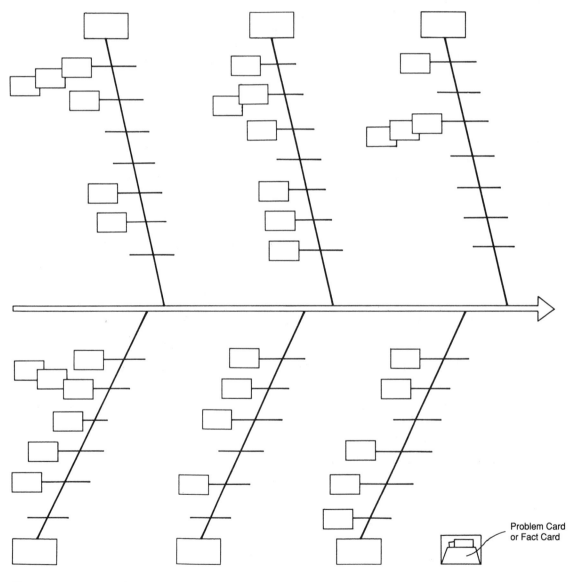

Figure 18. The Cause Side of the CEDAC Diagram

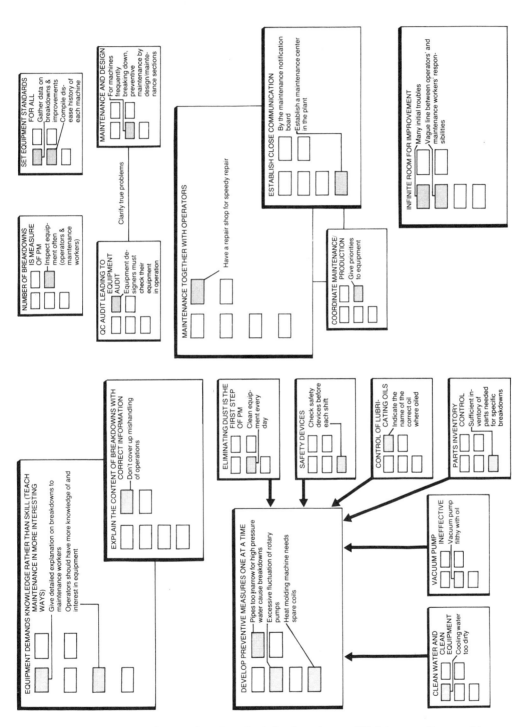

Figure 19. Some Ideas on TPM Developed on Cards by Operators and Maintenance Personnel in an Alloy Plant (300 Individuals Participated)

The cards must describe the facts as concretely as possible. Avoid abstract phrases using stereotyped expressions.

Cards should be added continuously until the target is attained. In other words, one try is not enough.

The leader must guide the others to fill in specific details adequately on the fact cards, leading them to "observe the facts more carefully."

Generate "Improvement Cards"

Gather the improvement cards and attach them to the right side of the spines on the Cause Side. Improvement cards are written in a short but detailed enough sentence to completely express an improvement idea for solving current problems and obstacles. The cards are written by all those involved in the project (e.g., managers, engineers, supervisors, and workers). They are all collected by the leader. The leader attaches the improvement cards onto the right side of the corresponding fact card. (Refer to Figure 20.)

The improvement cards are, in effect, a collection of all accumulated experience, as well as administrative knowledge and technical expertise. Therefore, the improvement cards reflect the level of daily study and efforts of the team. If there are two or more improvement cards for the same problem, they should all be attached to the diagram.

Add improvement cards continuously until the target is attained.

If the generation of improvement cards is sluggish, the leader should take the initiative to individually guide and encourage the team members to develop improvement ideas that take advantage of their respective strengths.

Test Improvement Ideas

Evaluate the substance of the improvement cards and put them into practice. Test results must be monitored on the Effect Side. The contents of each improvement card must be considered separately. A *red mark*, placed on the right side of the improvement card signifies that it has been selected. As a rule, selection is done at a meeting, according to the following criteria:

1. *Unusable*: Inadequate as improvement idea. Ineffective in solving the problem. *Do not place a mark on the card.*
2. *Of Interest*: Could be an effective improvement idea. However, among these, some might not be able to be implemented immediately because, for example, they require too much capital investment. *Place one red dot on the card.*
3. *Under Preparation*: This improvement idea will be used. Preparations for testing have begun: scheduling for tools and equipment modification, getting

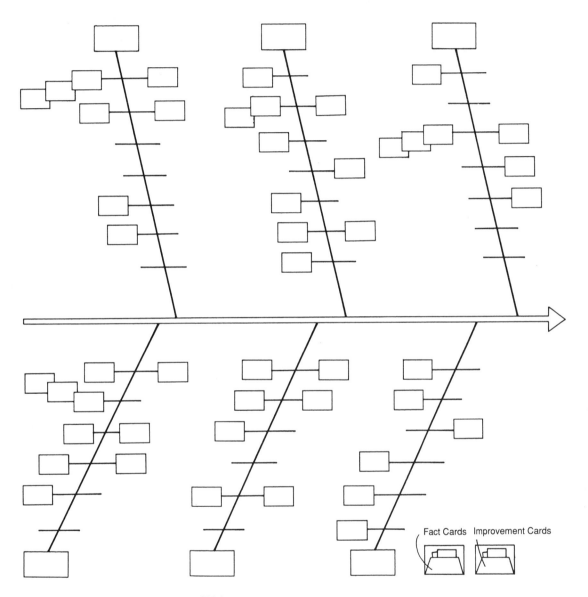

Figure 20. CEDAC Diagram (Cause Side)

necessary budget, and reviewing plans such as manning, training, and implementation date. *Place two red dots on the card.*

4. *Under Test*: This improvement idea is being tested, and the result is being monitored on the Effect Side. (Refer to Figure 22.) *Place three red dots on the card.* There are two ways of running tests:

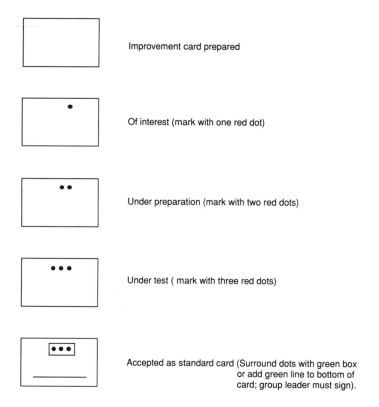

Figure 21. Improvement Card Acceptance Sequence

- Implementing each improvement idea sequentially and considering each result separately.
- Implementing several improvement ideas at once, and looking at the overall effect.

The appropriate approach depends on the content of the improvement ideas. When the opinions of the team members are split, the leader makes the final decision.

When the problem is simple, the fact card writing may be skipped, and you may start with the improvement cards. The purpose of writing the fact cards is to facilitate improvement ideas that are directly linked to the actual facts.

When the problem is complicated, it may be necessary to follow more step-by-step thinking processes and even to invent new categories such as those in Figure 23: "matters known," "questions," "matters to investigate," and "ideas for improvement."

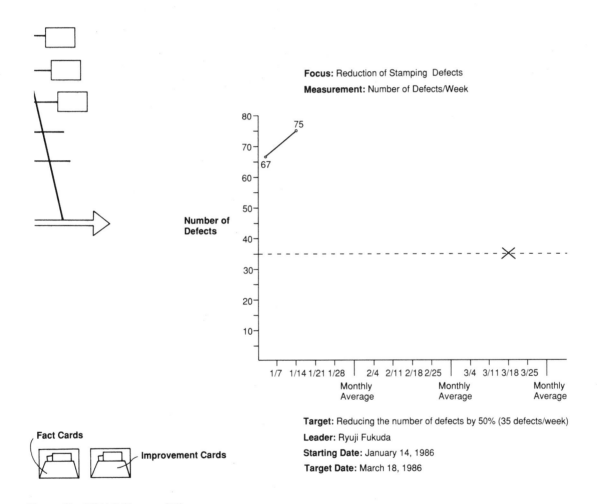

Focus: Reduction of Stamping Defects

Measurement: Number of Defects/Week

Number of Defects

Target: Reducing the number of defects by 50% (35 defects/week)

Leader: Ryuji Fukuda

Starting Date: January 14, 1986

Target Date: March 18, 1986

Fact Cards

Improvement Cards

Figure 22. CEDAC Diagram (#1)

Choose "Standard Cards"

Improvement cards with good results obtained on the Effect Side become "standard cards." If there is more than one improvement idea for a given problem, test each idea separately. Look at the results on the Effect Side. The ones with the best results

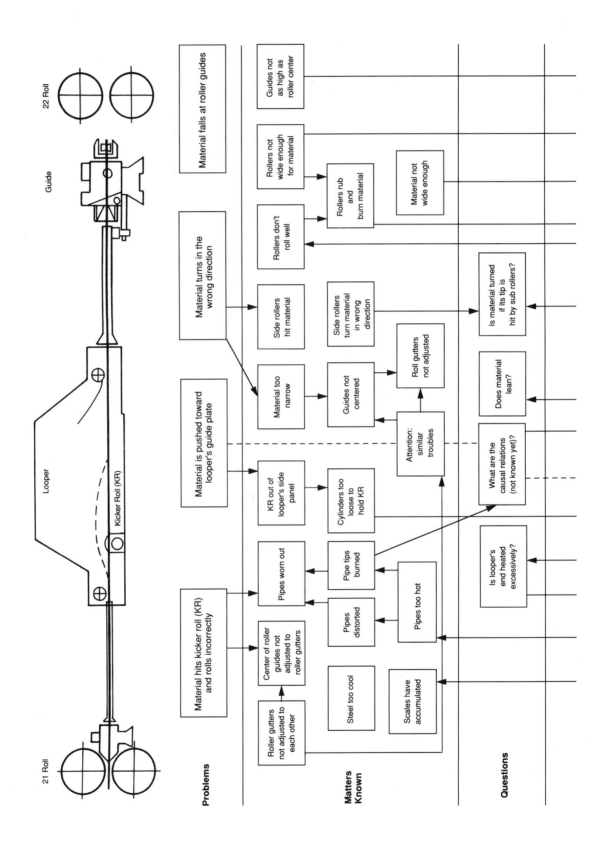

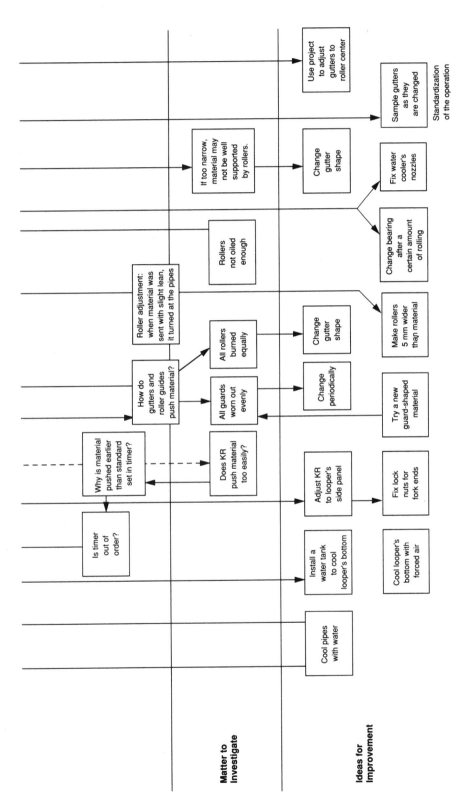

Figure 23. Workers List Problems Causing Defects in Rolled Steel Wire Operation: A CEDAC Approach

become standard cards. Either enclose the three dots by a green box, or draw a green line in highlighter on the bottom of the card. The leader makes this standard official by putting his signature on the card.

The standard card may be removed from the Cause Side and placed in a specific place on the upper right side of the CEDAC Diagram. (Refer to Figure 24.) It can also be placed in a transparent holder and hung conspicuously in the workplace.

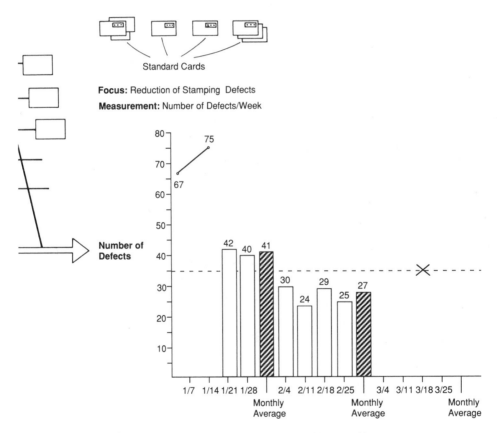

Figure 24. CEDAC Diagram (#2)

Traditionally, setting the standard was the job of several managers or engineers, and workers simply had to abide by the chosen standards. Unlike that approach, the CEDAC Diagram depends on everyone's participation to set the standard.

Furthermore, due to the nature of the CEDAC Diagram steps as explained, the standard set through this activity is not a static one — once set, never changed. Rather it is a living standard which is expected to be improved on a continuous basis. The CEDAC Diagram demonstrates in a tangible way that "improvement is an ongoing process, not one that ends."

Adhere to Standards

Know the standard and adhere to it. After following the previous steps until the standard is finally set, information about the new standard must be spread among those involved by means of the CEDAC Diagram. In effect, the Diagram becomes a Visual Controls System.

The members know the progress of the standardization procedure. Furthermore, they also know what impact the standard has on the Effect Side.

The details of the standard must be both known and adhered to by all individuals involved. A standard that evolves as the result of a collective effort is much easier to follow than one simply prescribed by management.

When the target on the Effect Side is attained, the standardization process pauses for the time being. In such a stage, it is advisable to keep only the necessary information near the workplace and roll up the CEDAC Diagram for storage. For example, the standard cards can be inserted in a transparent holder and displayed in a prominent place. When a new condition needing improvement emerges, the CEDAC Diagram can be taken out and used again in the same manner.

CHAPTER 4

Knowing and Adhering to the Standard (Right Method)

The last chapter reviewed the steps in making a CEDAC Diagram. The final step in that process is adhering to the standard. Window Development, discussed in this chapter, is a useful way to ensure that everyone understands and adheres to the right method.

Window Development Consists of Two Steps

Step One

In Table 5, five procedures are indicated. They are to be implemented in order as follows:

1. Concisely and concretely describe the defective outcome (what happened).
2. Describe the "unpracticed" factors concretely in terms of Party X and Party Y (what party did not do what). If nothing is unpracticed, leave the column blank.
3. Describe the "unknown" factors concretely in terms of Party X and Party Y (what party did not know what). If nothing is unknown, leave the column blank.
4. Write the contents of the day-to-day countermeasure to eliminate the "unpracticed" and "unknown" problems.
5. The person making the countermeasure evaluates its effectiveness. Completely effective measures receive 100 points. Completely ineffective measures receive 0 points. If its anticipated effectiveness is less than 70 points, the countermeasure should be reconsidered until it achieves a level of 70 or more points.

By practicing these procedures repeatedly, the "unpracticed" and "unknown" factors will be eliminated from daily work. Window Development provides a valuable step-by-step approach to attain perfect work.

Step Two

If the self-assessment of the effectiveness of the day-to-day countermeasure in Table 5 totals more than 70 points, progress to Table 6 and implement the countermeasure accordingly. When doing so, the countermeasure designer's immediate

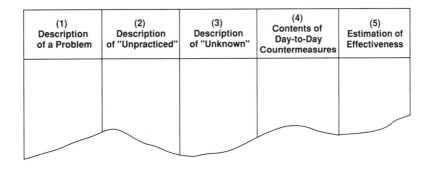

Table 5. Window Development (Step One)

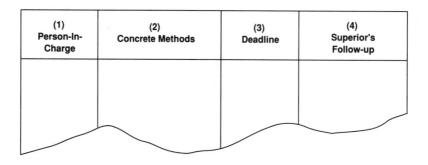

Table 6. Window Development (Step Two)

superior must follow the progress closely. He should check the results of the countermeasure and check whether the countermeasure is being performed properly as planned.

Inadequacies should be eradicated by on-the-job training, in which managers and supervisors guide and coach their subordinate personnel. The daily on-the-job training provided by the manager is the key to perfect implementation of the countermeasure.

Appendix

Analysis of the Effectiveness of the CEDAC System for Quality Problems

The following is an edited version of Dr. Ryuji Fukuda's paper, "The Application of the CEDAC for Standardization and Quality Control." It was published in the 1978 August-September issue of the publication, *Hyojunka to Hinshitsu kanri* (Standardization and Quality Control), of the Japan Standard Association. In the same year, it was awarded the Nikkei Prize for QC Papers by the Deming Prize Committee.

The paper analyzes the effectiveness of the CEDAC Diagram as applied to QC problems. Since it describes the important conditions for successful use of the CEDAC System, such as creating a favorable environment and using reliable management systems, it is hoped that the reader will use this appendix as a reference.

- Joharry's Window
- The New Joharry's Window
- Adhering to Established Standards and Finding New Methods
- Results and Their Time Periods
- Four Measures for Analysis
- Relationships Between Factors and Results
- Conclusions of the Analysis

Joharry's Window

Table 7 summarizes the results obtained in two plants where the CEDAC Diagram was used plant-wide and applied to a total of thirty-one quality defect reduction targets. The results were obtained within periods of four days to eight months. In about half of the cases, defects decreased by more than 90%, far surpassing our original expectations.

As Figure 25 shows, Joharry's Window was used by Joseph Ruft and Harry Ingram to describe communication between two people. Though Ruft and Ingram used this figure to explain internal mental processes, it gave us a clue to the cause of CEDAC's effectiveness.

1. In Categories II and III, there is an obvious need to clarify and exchange information. According to the CEDAC System, "I" and "You" shift from Categories II and III to Category I by increasing the area of common knowledge.
2. Upon examining several cases where the CEDAC Diagram had been applied, we found that in some cases the communication of the existence of Category II

and III conditions was by itself enough to achieve results. However, in other cases, shifting from Categories II and III to Category I conditions did not result in the desired change. When this is the case, one must tackle Category IV, namely currently unknown factors, by discovering possible technical causes and equipment problems, and by developing new methods.

3. In the past, most of the quality improvement activities have been a search into Category IV. At times, however, they were made before a shift from Categories II and III to Category I was attempted, if even considered.

   On some occasions, if the root of the problem was uncovered, results would improve. However, in other cases, when the improvement measures resulted in a sluggish effect due to the unstable and undefined elements in Categories II and III, it was quite possible we misjudged the situation. Or, even when right measures were taken, notable results would not be achieved.

4. Before the use of the CEDAC System, we observed cases in which a new method had temporarily improved the situation greatly, but had soon returned to the original level. One cause of this was an incomplete transition from Categories II and III to Category I.

   On the other hand, perhaps the shift to Category I had been complete at a certain point, but with time, the changing environment had forced it back to Categories II and III. In other words, unless the effort to transfer Category II and III conditions to Category I is exerted on a day-to-day basis, there is no guarantee that Category I conditions will remain.

   In this regard, what makes the CEDAC Diagram significant lies in the following points: (1) all individuals involved can refer to the diagram at any time, and (2) standards are revised by the on-going and simple process of adding new cards to the diagram.

5. Although improvements in technique and equipment may be central to solving QC problems, the shift from Categories II and III to Category I is crucial as a groundwork for success.

The New Joharry's Window

Quality control is based on close observation of the facts during daily production activities. Furthermore, by trial-and-error repetition in production activities, knowledge and competence in quality improvement accumulates.

There appear many cases that cannot be explained merely by the hypothesis of Joharry's Window. Obviously, that one "knows" something does not necessarily

Results / Defects	◎	○	△	Total Number of Defects
Number of Defects	16	10	5	31
Percentage of Defects	52%	32%	16%	100%

Key:

◎ More than 90% decrease in defects

○ 50-90% decrease in defects

△ Less than 50% decrease in defects

Table 7. CEDAC Results

I / You	Know	Don't Know
Know	I	II
Don't Know	III	IV

Figure 25. Joharry's Window

mean he "practices" it. A new window expands the original Joharry's Window by dividing the "known" category into "known-practiced" and "known-unpracticed." This is illustrated in Figure 26.

To solve any quality problem, one must progress through the whole cycle: (1) → (2) → (3) → (4) → (1). In other words, if any one of the steps is skipped, true resolution of the problem will not be possible.

The CEDAC Diagram is a useful tool to insure rotation of the cycle.

Adhering to the operational standards does not mean to treat them as rules to follow blindly. What is important is to question the standards (even if this results in occasional failure) so as to achieve constant overall improvement.

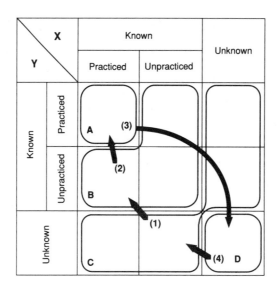

Figure 26. New Joharry's Window

In the beginning, the window was simply a way to explain the phenomena. However, later, we developed a method to use the window for analyzing problems. We call this "Window Analysis."

Adhering to Established Standards and Finding New Methods

Two Approaches to Solving Quality Problems

In the new Joharry's Window the measures for solving quality problems are broadly divided into two approaches: Category A (adhering to the established standard) and Category D (finding new and better operational and manufacturing methods).

The basic point in the hypothesis of the new Joharry's window is to "establish Category A first." If the problem remains unsolved, one should "turn to Category D."

Figure 27 classifies the results of 86 CEDAC cases, over a fixed time, into two groups:

1. Groups which focused their efforts only on "adhering to established standards."
2. Groups which succeeded in finding new methods.

The graphs demonstrate the importance of the discovery of new methods. However, when the groups that focus their efforts on discovering new methods were divided into two categories, we discovered another interesting fact. (Figure 28)

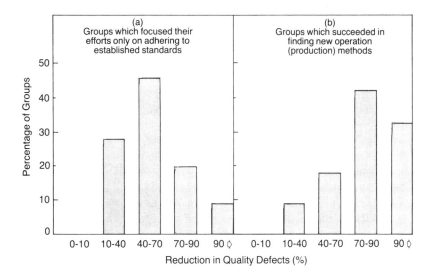

Figure 27. **Effectiveness of Finding New Methods Versus Adhering to Established Standards**

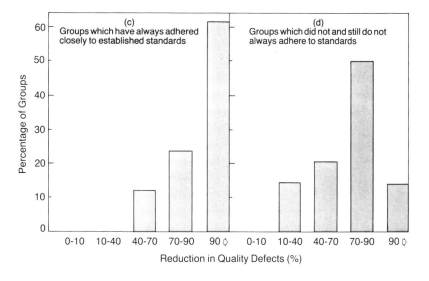

Figure 28. **Groups Which Found Effective New Methods as a Direct Result of CEDAC**

Even after new improved methods have been found, there is a large difference in results between groups that have always adhered to established standards and those that have not. As in Figure 27, the better the adherence to standards, the more successful the project.

When the two approaches are compared, the direct effectiveness of "adherence to established standards" is smaller than that of "finding new methods." However, adherence increases a chance of finding new methods, as well as enhances the effect of the methods when they are established.

Necessary Conditions for Adhering to the Established Standards and Finding New Methods

Next, we searched for the necessary conditions for adhering to the established standards and finding new methods. The results of analysis show that in both cases the CEDAC System itself played an extremely influential role.

Figure 29 contrasts the factors which differed between the groups that had found new effective manufacturing methods and those that had not. (Note 1)
Groups that had

- adhered to former standards
- gathered workers' opinions and ideas well
- held active discussions, and
- constantly examined and revised the CEDAC Diagram

seemed to be more successful in discovering new production methods.

Furthermore, groups that succeeded in finding new production methods tended to provide thorough guidance and training for the newly-found methods. In other words, after being successful in Category D, they would strive to attain Category A status again.

Figure 30 illustrates the factors which influence the adherence to standards. Groups that had

- held frequent discussions
- gathered workers' opinions and ideas well
- strived to use concrete expressions on cards
- had worker participation in drawing up the CEDAC Diagram

were clearly more successful in adhering to the established standards.

It should be noted that this information, drawn from actual cases, shows quantitatively how essential it is to have both the participation of all persons concerned as well as mutual trust among all of the members. Together these promote the

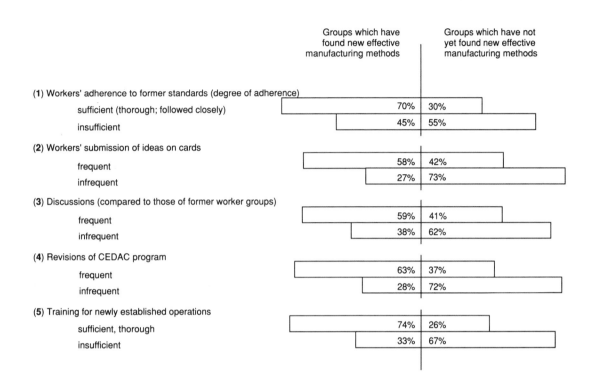

Figure 29. Factors for Finding New Methods

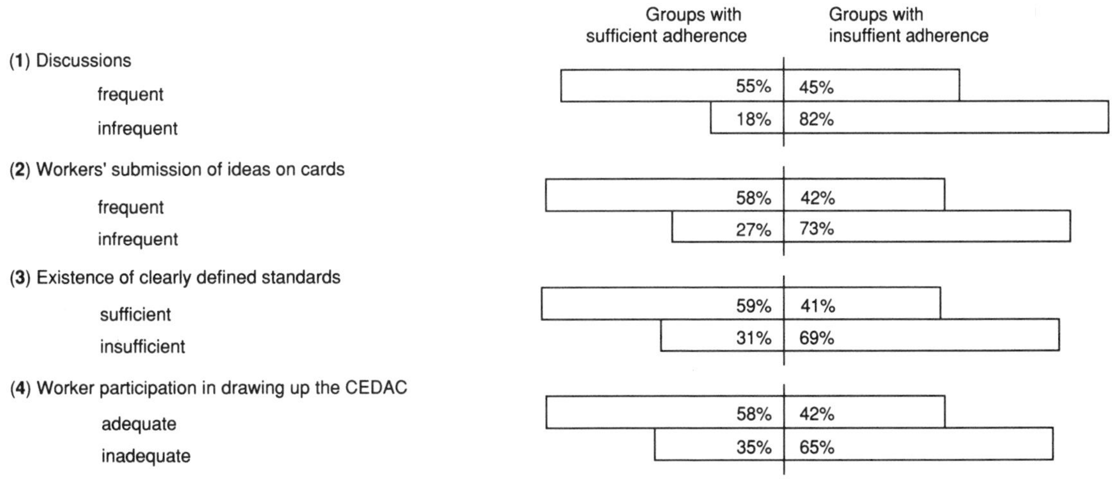

Figure 30. Factors for Adhering to Standards

adherence to standards and the constant development of improved methods for solving quality problems.

Results and Their Time Periods

Next, the time taken to achieve results was considered as a factor. The 86 groups were divided into four types according to the relationship between the time taken to achieve the results and the results themselves. The four types were as follows:

- quick but limited
- slow and limited
- quick and considerable
- slow but considerable

"Quick" refers to a time span of less that three months. "Limited" means a reduction of defects of less than 40%.

Figure 31 lists five countermeasures. It shows the percentage of the groups, within each type, which used a particular countermeasure effectively for their success.

For example, in the first item, 68% of the "quick and considerable" type groups indicated that one of their effective countermeasures was "visual display of key operational points."

The following can be observed from Figure 31:

1. Among the group of "quick and considerable," many thought that countermeasures 1, 2, and 3 were effective. These are the measures that ensure adherence to standards.
2. Among the groups of "slow but considerable," many indicated that in addition to countermeasures 1 and 3, they found countermeasures 4 and 5 effective for achieving the results. These measures are for finding new methods.

In summary, the "quick and considerable" type achieves the results through adhering to the established standards, while, the "slow but considerable" succeeds by finding new methods as well as adhering to the standards.

It can be concluded from the above analysis and from those in former sections that the following approach to solving quality problems is the most effective.

First, enforce adherence to the established standards. Unless the present operation and production methods themselves have a critical weakness, this approach alone leads to quick and considerable reduction of defects.

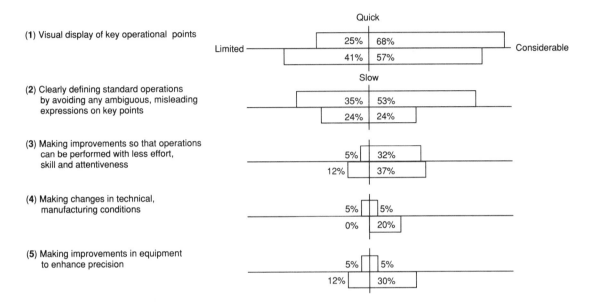

Figure 31. Countermeasures Identified as Effective

In cases in which the defects still remain, work on developing new operation and production methods. The data show that if adherence to standards is established, it increases a chance of finding new methods and enhances the effectiveness of the newly discovered methods.

These conclusions are consistent with the hypothesis of the New Joharry's Window.

Four Measures for Analysis

Creating a CEDAC Model

We developed a model that could predict the results of CEDAC activities of individual factors. In doing so, we took all the many influential factors into consideration.

These steps are illustrated in Figure 32 (Note 2). The goals can be summarized in two points:

1. In order to attain the most desirable results in a given environment, the CEDAC model decides how individual factors should be controlled.

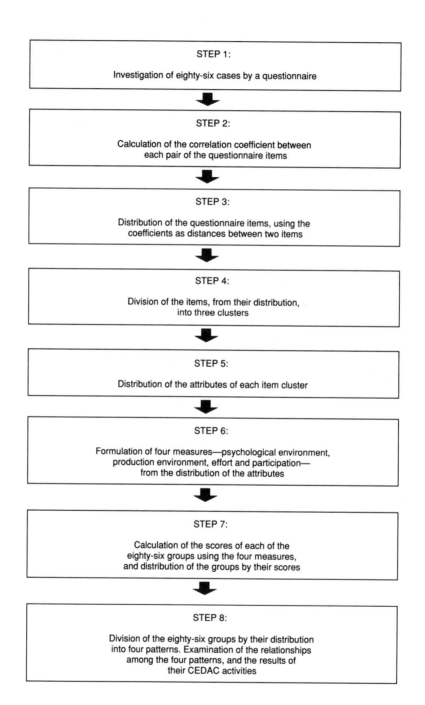

Figure 32. Formulation of the CEDAC Model

2. The CEDAC model can predict the results of ongoing processes. For example, if a bad result is foreseen, an action that will ameliorate the results can be taken.

Grouping of the Questionnaire Items

Twenty-three items were selected from the questionnaire which could affect the results of the CEDAC activity. Each item was paired with each of the other 22 items, and a correlation coefficient was calculated for each pair. (Note 3) Using these coefficients, all items were plotted out in a two-dimensional plane so that the items closely related would cluster together as in Figure 33. (Note 4)

In Figure 33, on the right side, there appear "frequency of appearance of defects," "frequency of operations with defects," etc. These items refer to the production environment in which groups tackled their own problems.

In the lower left are items such as "concern of managers," "morale for solving problems," etc. These items are associated with the psychological environment of the plants. And in the upper left appear "submission of ideas on cards," "revision of the diagram," etc., which are items related to the use of the CEDAC Diagram. So, it is observed that these 23 items can be divided into three groups — the production environment, the psychological environment, and the use of the CEDAC Diagram.

Formulation of Four Measures from the Questionnaire Items

In the preceding section, the 23 questionnaire items were divided into three clusters. In the next step, 3 to 5 alternative answers (let us call them "attributes") to each questionnaire item were placed on a two-dimensional plane so that the closer two attributes were related, the nearer they were located. (Note 5) This distribution was made separately for each of the three clusters.

Production environment

Figure 34 shows that the attributes representing the good aspects of the production environment are situated on the right side and those representing the poor aspects on the left. Let us call the groups having good attributes (on the right side) A-type, and those having poor attributes B-type. The two types are compared in Table 8.

The A-type groups are managed well. They had already solved most problems before their CEDAC activities and could go on to deal with ones which were left unsolved.

B-type seemed busy in production work, which left little time for management, and left big problems unsolved in their routine operation.

Thus, the X-axis in Figure 34 can be interpreted to indicate the quality of the production environment. Figure 35 shows the values of the attributes in reference

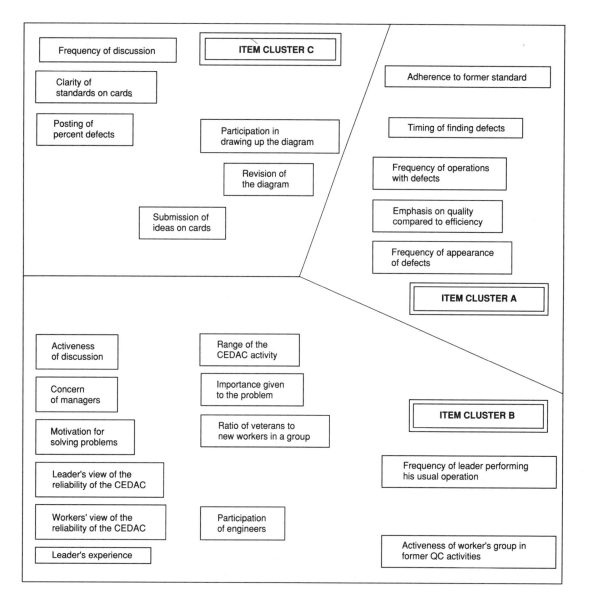

Figure 33. Distribution of the Questionnaire Items into Two-Dimensional Space

to the X-axis. If the values are more to the plus side, the attributes represented by them are more favorable in terms of the production environment.

It should be noted that the most favorable attribute of a production environment is "sufficient adherence to former standards."

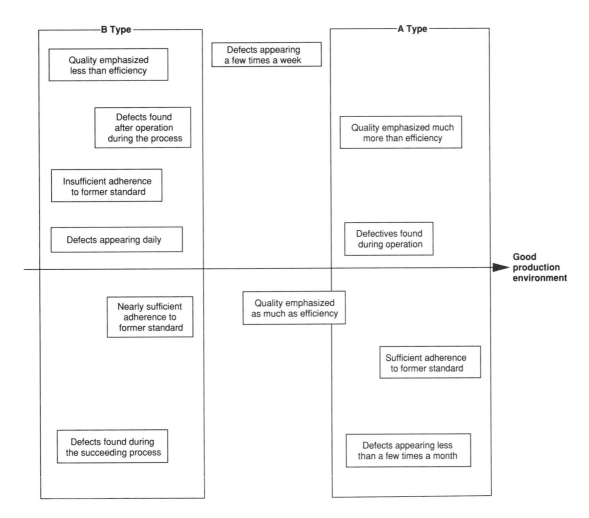

Figure 34. Distribution of the Attributes of Item Cluster A: Production Environment

The second most favorable is "emphasis of quality compared to efficiency." Among the necessary plant management indexes such as quality, due date, and efficiency, those groups that had a good production environment put top priority on quality. Having concrete measurements under the quality-first policy, their day-to-day factory operations were carried out.

When an item of the questionnaire commands a wide range of values from plus to minus, it has a greater influence over the production environment.

The significant point is that we could obtain such clear results from our own actual cases. With these results in mind, we can access the situation in quantitative weight using available information.

B Type groups in a poor production environment	A Type groups in a good production environment
• Emphasize efficiency rather than quality • Have insufficient adherence to standards • Have defects frequently • Cannot locate defects during operation	• Emphasize quality above all • Have sufficient adherence to standards • Have defects infrequently • Can locate defects during operation

Table 8. Production Environment

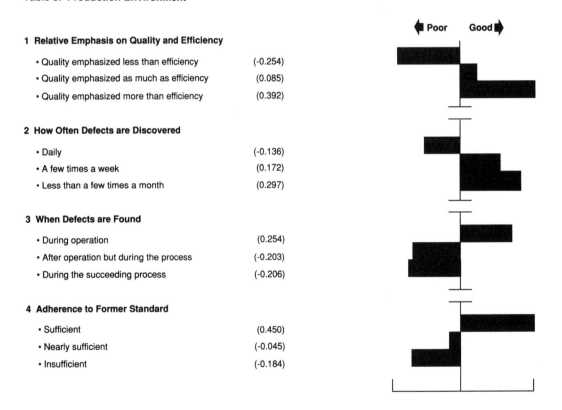

1 Relative Emphasis on Quality and Efficiency

• Quality emphasized less than efficiency	(-0.254)
• Quality emphasized as much as efficiency	(0.085)
• Quality emphasized more than efficiency	(0.392)

2 How Often Defects are Discovered

• Daily	(-0.136)
• A few times a week	(0.172)
• Less than a few times a month	(0.297)

3 When Defects are Found

• During operation	(0.254)
• After operation but during the process	(-0.203)
• During the succeeding process	(-0.206)

4 Adherence to Former Standard

• Sufficient	(0.450)
• Nearly sufficient	(-0.045)
• Insufficient	(-0.184)

Figure 35. Scores of the Attributes of Production Environment

Psychological environment

The distribution of the attributes of the 12 questions pertaining to the psychological environment is shown in Figure 36. Here again, the attributes group which seemed to affect the outcomes favorably (A-type) appears on the right side and the unfavorable group (B-type) appears on the left. The comparison of the two is in Table 9.

B Type groups in a poor psychological environment	A Type groups in a good psychological environment
• Are directed by managers with little concern	• Are directed by managers with much concern
• Have leaders and workers who do not feel the CEDAC to be reliable	• Have leaders and workers who feel the CEDAC to be reliable
• Have not been actively dealing with problems in their group activities	• Have been very actively dealing with problems in their group activities
• Are tackling problems deemed unimportant	• Are tackling problems deemed important
• Have low motivation for solving their problems	• Have high motivation for solving their problems
• Have discussions as inactive as ever in spite of the CEDAC	• Have discussion more active than ever through using the CEDAC
• Are in plants where only one or a few groups are using the CEDAC	• Are in plants where all groups are using the CEDAC
• Have leaders who do not perform their ordinary operation	• Have leaders who perform their ordinary operation as much as other workers
• Have less experienced leaders	• Have the most experienced leaders

Table 9. Psychological Environment

The degree of influence which each attribute has on the psychological environment is shown by Figure 37. It can be observed that those having a relatively strong influence are:

• leader's knowledge and experience
• motivation for solving problems
• leader's and workers' view of CEDAC's reliability
• concern of managers

Use of CEDAC

Distribution was made of 23 attributes (from 6 questionnaire items) as to the use of CEDAC. The results are shown in Figure 38. In the case of the production of psychological environment, there appeared only one axis which indicated the quality of the environments.

In the case of the use of CEDAC, however, favorable attributes were concentrated in the upper right hand side. From this, it was reasoned that both the horizontal and vertical axes had something unknown which would be interesting to study further.

By careful comparison of attributes in the upper and lower sides as well as those at the left and right, we thought it safe to conclude that the horizontal represents participation, and the vertical represents efforts. The comparison of each type

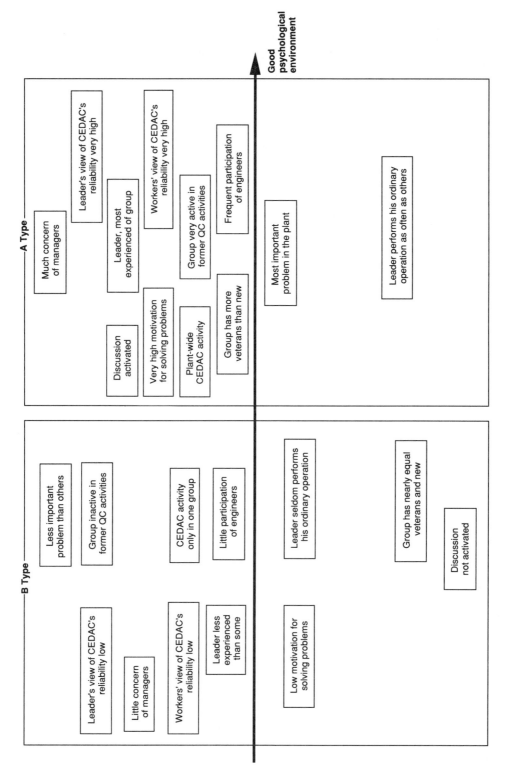

Figure 36. Distribution of the Attributes of Item Cluster B: Psychological Environment

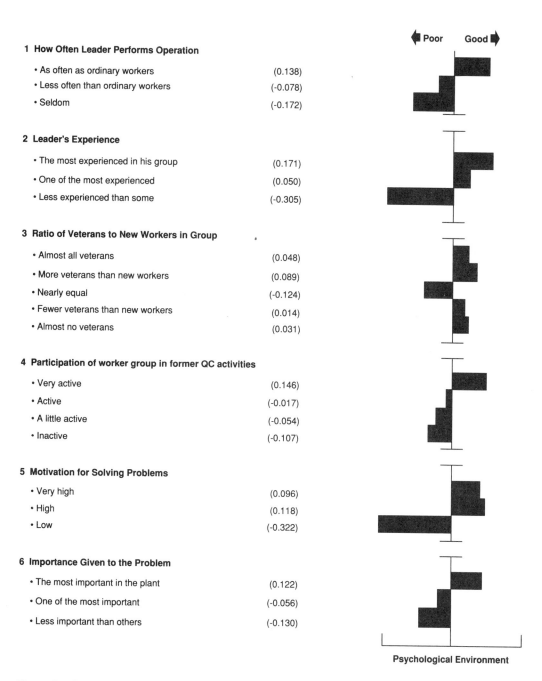

1 How Often Leader Performs Operation

• As often as ordinary workers	(0.138)
• Less often than ordinary workers	(-0.078)
• Seldom	(-0.172)

2 Leader's Experience

• The most experienced in his group	(0.171)
• One of the most experienced	(0.050)
• Less experienced than some	(-0.305)

3 Ratio of Veterans to New Workers in Group

• Almost all veterans	(0.048)
• More veterans than new workers	(0.089)
• Nearly equal	(-0.124)
• Fewer veterans than new workers	(0.014)
• Almost no veterans	(0.031)

4 Participation of worker group in former QC activities

• Very active	(0.146)
• Active	(-0.017)
• A little active	(-0.054)
• Inactive	(-0.107)

5 Motivation for Solving Problems

• Very high	(0.096)
• High	(0.118)
• Low	(-0.322)

6 Importance Given to the Problem

• The most important in the plant	(0.122)
• One of the most important	(-0.056)
• Less important than others	(-0.130)

Poor ◄ Good ►

Psychological Environment

Figure 37. Scores of the Attributes of Psychological Environment

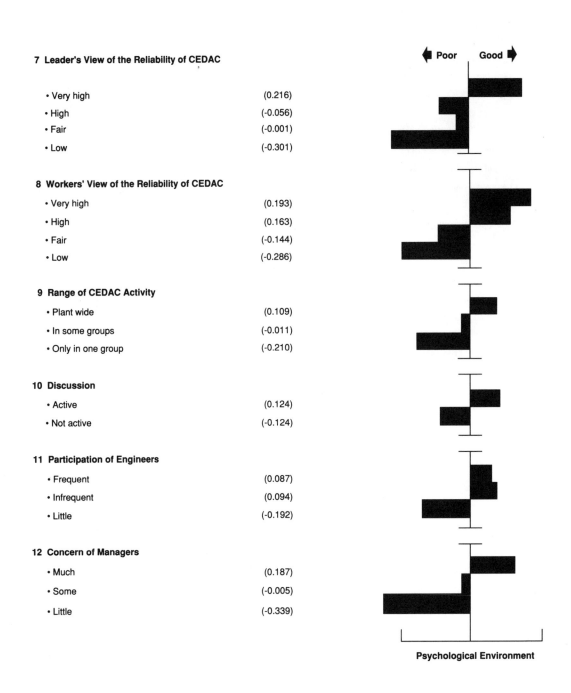

7 Leader's View of the Reliability of CEDAC

• Very high	(0.216)
• High	(-0.056)
• Fair	(-0.001)
• Low	(-0.301)

8 Workers' View of the Reliability of CEDAC

• Very high	(0.193)
• High	(0.163)
• Fair	(-0.144)
• Low	(-0.286)

9 Range of CEDAC Activity

• Plant wide	(0.109)
• In some groups	(-0.011)
• Only in one group	(-0.210)

10 Discussion

• Active	(0.124)
• Not active	(-0.124)

11 Participation of Engineers

• Frequent	(0.087)
• Infrequent	(0.094)
• Little	(-0.192)

12 Concern of Managers

• Much	(0.187)
• Some	(-0.005)
• Little	(-0.339)

Poor   Good

Psychological Environment

Figure 37. Scores of the Attributes of Psychological Environment (cont'd)

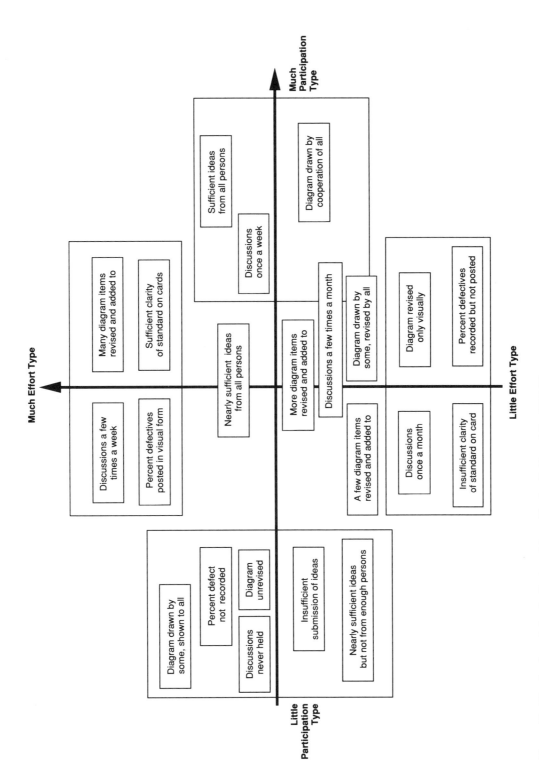

Figure 38. Distribution of the Attributes of Item Cluster C: Use of the CEDAC

is made in Table 10. "Participation" refers to a successful situation involving all people concerned. "Effort" refers to a situation where a few people, possibly foremen and production engineers, work very hard and sustain the improvement activities.

Relationships Between Factors and Results

Using the four axes — production environment, psychological environment, participation, and effort — the CEDAC activity of a group can be described numerically.

In other words, the CEDAC activities of 86 groups are represented by dots in four-dimensional space. In order to make the cluster of the dots visually clear, they are projected on a plane so that the distance between every two dots is expressed as accurately as possible, as shown in Figure 39. This makes it possible for groups whose scoring patterns are similar to each other to be located in close proximity. (Note 6)

Since the objects of the model are human activities which are products of innumerable factors, it is impossible to predict their results as clearly as in the case of physical phenomena. However, there appeared, although not very distinctly, four

Little Participation Type	Much Participation Type
• Use diagrams drawn only by a few	• Use diagrams drawn through the cooperation of all
• Have no discussion	• Have discussion once a week
• Have insufficient submission of ideas on cards	• Have sufficient submission of ideas on cards from all persons

Little Effort Type	Much Effort Type
• Revise the diagrams only into a more visual form	• Revise the contents of the diagrams and add cards to many items
• Have discussion once a month	• Have discussion a few times a week
• Standards written on cards unclearly	• Standards written on cards clearly
• Record their percent defects but do not post them	• Post their percent defects in visual form

Table 10. Use of the CEDAC

patterns of the CEDAC activities. Further, we examined how successful the groups of each pattern were in finding methods and in achieving sufficient adherence. As a result, it became clear that a group's success is closely related to the patterns of the group to which it belongs. Table 11 is a list of the characteristics of each pattern described below:

Pattern A

Having better environments, both the participation and the effort were good. The groups were successful both in finding new methods and in achieving sufficient adherence. The results were highly satisfactory. Where quick and considerable results were obtained, almost all cases fell exclusively in this pattern.

Pattern B

The environments were both poor. Not much extra time was left for problem-solving efforts. Nevertheless, CEDAC activity was carried out with much participation. Finding methods was difficult in this pattern, but sufficient adherence was easily attained. Fair results were achieved.

Pattern C

Working under a fairly good environment, though not as good as A, much effort was expended in trying to solve their problems. They were often successful in finding new effective methods but adherence was not good, probably because of limited participation. The results were fair or considerable, but slow.

Pattern D

Both the production and the psychological environment were poor. Neither participation nor effort was sufficient. The overall results were poor.

From all that has been mentioned above, the following can be learned in regard to CEDAC activity:

1. The group having a good environment should aim at Pattern A in Table 11. If, like in Pattern C, only a handful of people work hard to find new methods, a longer time will be needed.
2. Those who are in poor environments should direct themselves to Pattern B which emphasizes participation, although they may not have much spare time to devote to their problems. However unfavorable the environments are, participation is possible. Fair results can be expected in a short period of time with complete adherence. By improving the environments through full participation

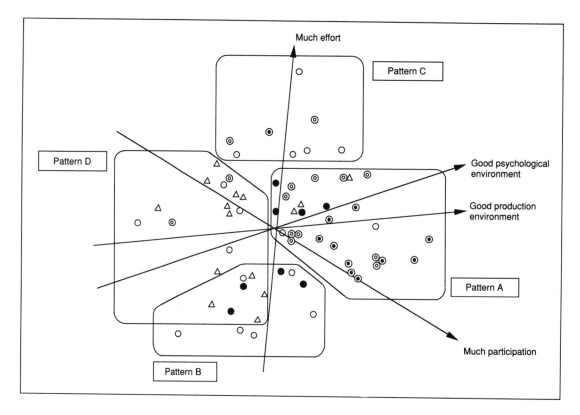

Figure 39. Patterns of Groups and Results

according to Pattern B, they will one day make a breakthrough into Pattern A performance.

In Figure 39, plottings to show the groups which could produce only limited results within three months are omitted. However, from their answers to the questionnaire, we calculated their scores for the four axes, and forecast the results as being either slow-but-considerable, or slow-and-limited.

Conclusions of the Analysis

This analysis is based on the data from 86 cases of CEDAC application, or rather on the results of experiments conducted by 86 groups.

These results shed light on the existence of vital points underlying not only CEDAC activities but also any form of improvement activities one may carry out.

	Production Environment	Psychological Environment	Participation	Effort	Finding New Methods	Adherence to Standards	Results
A	○	○	○	○	○	○	○ ◎ ●
B	×	×	○	×	×	○	● ○
C	○	○	×	○	○	×	◎ ○
D	×	×	×	×	×	×	○ △

Symbols of Results

Time Period	Percentage of Quality Defects Reduction		
	0 - 40%	40% - 70%	70% and above
Less than 3 Months		●	◉
3 Months or More	△	○	◎

Table 11. Four Patterns of Groups

The following two points outline newly-acquired knowledge as a result of this study:

1. It has generally been understood that for solving quality problems, there is a series of steps to be followed. They are analysis, improvement, standardization, and adherence. In the above study it has been proven that adherence is not only a means to achieve quick and considerable results, but also it is a springboard for improvement (finding methods). Adherence is also an element that ensures and increases the effectiveness of newly discovered methods. In other words, we should go around the circle in Figure 40 from complete adherence to the manufacturing and operational methods that are already known. This must be repeated until satisfactory results are obtained.

2. In the past, each of us might have felt that we had to make a choice between the school in favor of "participation and discussion" and the school of "down-right elimination of quality defects" which considered the former bothersome. But now, the data we have obtained show that these two can be fully integrated. The participation of all persons concerned is indispensable in achieving complete adherence as well as in finding new methods. It is wrong to eliminate participation and discussion just because it takes too much time. They are necessary to

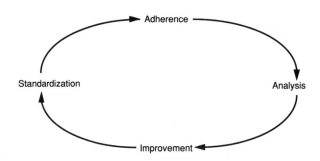

Figure 40.

bring about solutions in a short period of time. This has been proven in our efforts to solve quality problems. As a final remark, it should be added that participation and discussion are most effective when directed toward reaching a clear-cut, concrete objective.

Notes

Notes

Note 1

Figures 28 and 29 were compiled as seen in the following:

Discussion \ Adherence	Sufficient	Insufficient	Total
Frequent	20	46	66
Infrequent	1	14	15
Total	21	60	81

Table A. Original data (Number of groups)

Discussion \ Adherence	Sufficient	Insufficient	Total
Frequent	95	77	172
Infrequent	5	23	28
Total	100	100	200

Table B. The number of groups is set at 100 each for both "sufficient" and "insufficient adherence"

Discussion \ Adherence	Sufficient	Insufficient	Total
Frequent	55%	45%	100%
Infrequent	18%	82%	100%

Table C. Percentages obtained from Table B (above)

Discussion \ Adherence	Sufficient	Insufficient	Total
Frequent	30%	70%	100%
Infrequent	7%	93%	100%

Table D. Percentages obtained directly from the original data

The reason for establishing the number 100 in Table B is that the degree of adherence is relative. The percentage ratio can vary according to the yardstick. Therefore, looking at D, if one says that, although frequent discussions were held, the rate of adherence is a mere 30% and therefore not sufficient, it is wrong. If we assume that there is no relation between the amount of discussion and the degree of adherence, the four frames of Table C have to be filled in at 50%. The point here is that if there were not enough discussions, the possibility of achieving sufficient adherence drops from the originally possible 50% to 18%. (On the other hand, no assurance can be given for sufficient adherence even if there were enough discussions. The discussion is a necessary condition for adherence but not the sole condition.)

Note 2

We did not establish a hypothesis when we formulated the model. The relationships between factors and results become clear as we grouped the closely related factors together. We let the data speak for themselves, and then summed up the results which produced the model. Therefore the model is highly reliable since it is not bound by any given premises.

Note 3

Cramer's coefficient of contingency was used for the correlation coefficient. This coefficient represents the closeness of relations among items shown by the numerals between 0 and 1. If no positive relations are observed, as in the case of Table E, the coefficient is 0. If, as in F, two items are completely related to each other, then, the coefficient is 1.

Item 1 \ Item 2	Yes	No	Total
Yes	5	5	10
No	5	5	10
Total	10	10	20

Item 1 \ Item 2	Yes	No	Total
Yes	10	0	10
No	0	10	10
Total	10	10	20

Table E. Unrelated items: coefficient = 0   **Table F. Related items: coefficient = 1**

Note 4

Hayashi's quantification theory IV was used. Assume there are 4 samples, and the distances between the samples are known. Then, using a three-dimensional space, the 4 samples can be given their correct positions according to the known distances. Likewise, if the number of samples is n, you need n-1 dimensional space. However, we cannot visualize this dimension. So, we pick a plane on which we can reproduce, as correctly as possible, the distances between the samples, and project each point of the n-1 dimensional space on the plane. The figure below is the result of this process where a visible space arrangement is obtained. Figure 33 is obtained in this manner.

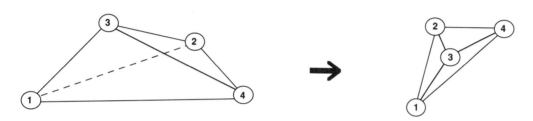

Figure A.

Note 5

Hayashi's quantification theory III was used. Suppose we received answers to the questionnaire as shown below.

Item Groups	1. Discussion		2. Morale for Solving Problems	
	Frequent	Infrequent	High	Low
A	√		√	
B	√		√	
		√		√

Table G.

If several groups answer that they had frequent discussions and also had high motivation for solving problems, then it is reasonable to suspect that the two attributes, "having frequent discussions" and "having high motivation for solving problems" are related in some way. Thus, those groups giving similar answers, Group A and Group B, would appear to be alike. The object of Theory III is to arrange these related groups and items closely together.

Note 6

Principal component analysis (PCA) was used. When there are many measures like x1, x2, x3, etc. they can be condensed into a smaller number of measures using PCA. The following illustrates:

$$Z = \alpha_1 X_1 + \alpha_2 X_2 + \alpha_3 X_3 \ldots$$

$$Z = \beta_1 X_1 + \beta_2 X_2 + \beta_3 X_3 \ldots$$

For example, when there are two measures to be condensed into one, PCA makes a new axis so that the distances between the samples are shown as accurately as possible, as follows (p.131):

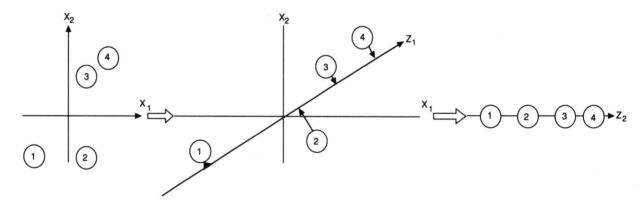

Figure B.

About the Author

Ryuji Fukuda is one of the world's most highly qualified experts in the field of industrial engineering, stockless production, and quality improvement. After a brilliant career with leading Japanese firms, including nearly 30 years at Sumitomo Electric, he is now serving as a consultant to the Japan Management Association and to major firms in Japan, North America, and Europe (including Fiat, Michelin, Philips, Volvo). In 1978 he was honored with the prestigious Japanese Deming Prize for his contribution in the field of productivity and quality improvement. He is the author of numerous publications pertaining to production management, including *Managerial Engineering* published by Productivity Press in 1983. He teaches courses in Quality Assurance at the University of Kobe.

CEDAC Analysis Forms

The following pages contain blank forms for preparing window analyses and for setting up the effect side of your CEDAC diagram. Make photocopies to use for problem analysis in the future.

Included with this book is a sample CEDAC chart to help you get started with your first CEDAC analysis. Good luck!

	Know	Don't Know
You: I / Know		
Know		
Don't Know		

Joharry's Window

	Know	Don't Know
You: I / Know		
Know		
Don't Know		

Joharry's Window

You \ I	Know	Don't Know
Know		
Don't Know		

Joharry's Window

You \ I	Know	Don't Know
Know		
Don't Know		

Joharry's Window

X / Y	Known		Unknown
	Practiced	Unpracticed	
Known Practiced	1	4	7
Known Unpracticed	2	5	8
Unknown	3	6	9

The Nine Window Frames

X Y	Known		Unknown
	Practiced	Unpracticed	
Known / Practiced	1	4	7
Known / Unpracticed	2	5	8
Unknown	3	6	9

The Nine Window Frames

X / Y	Known		Unknown
	Practiced	Unpracticed	
Known — Practiced	1	4	7
Known — Unpracticed	2	5	8
Unknown	3	6	9

The Nine Window Frames

Focus:

Measurement:

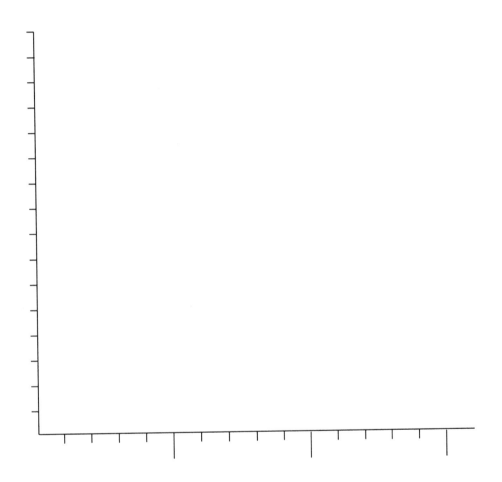

Target:
Leader:
Starting Date:
Target Date:

The Effect Side of the CEDAC Diagram

Focus:

Measurement:

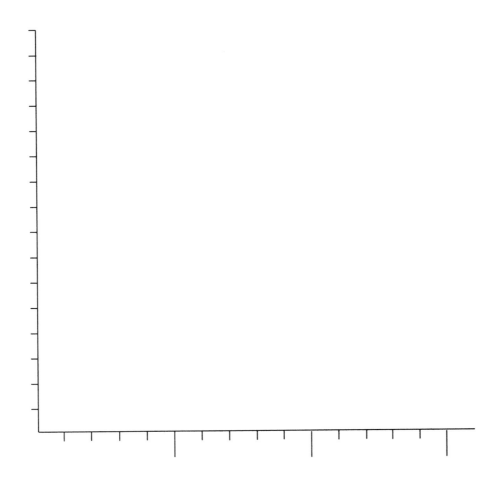

Target:

Leader:

Starting Date:

Target Date:

The Effect Side of the CEDAC Diagram

Focus:

Measurement:

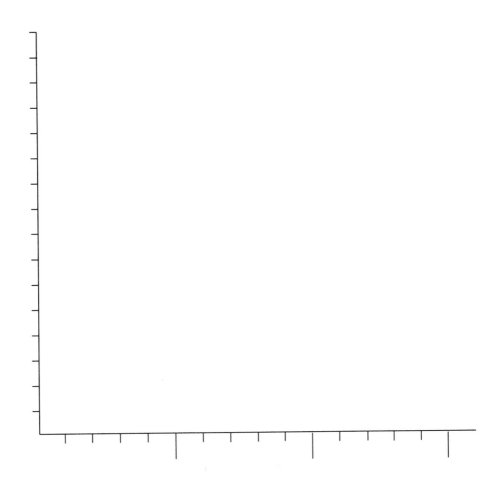

Target:
Leader:
Starting Date:
Target Date:

The Effect Side of the CEDAC Diagram

OTHER BOOKS ON CONTINUOUS IMPROVEMENT

Productivity Press publishes and distributes materials on continuous improvement in productivity, quality, customer service, and the creative involvement of all employees. Many of our products are direct source materials from Japan that have been translated into English for the first time and are available exclusively from Productivity. Supplemental products and services include newsletters, conferences, seminars, in-house training and consulting, audio-visual training programs, and industrial study missions. Call 1-800-274-9911 for our free book catalog.

Quality Function Deployment
Integrating Customer Requirements into Product Design
edited by Yoji Akao

      More and more, companies are using quality function deployment, or QFD, to identify their customers' requirements, translate them into quantified quality characteristics and then build them into their products and services. This casebook introduces the concept of quality deployment as it has been applied in a variety of industries in Japan. The materials include numerous case studies illustrating QFD applications. Written by the creator of QFD, this book provides direct source material on Quality Function Deployment, one of the essential tools for world class manufacturing. It is a design approach based on the idea that quality is determined by the customer. Through methodology and case studies the book offers insight into how Japanese companies identify customer requirements and describes how to translate customer requirements into qualified quality characteristics, and how to build them into products and services.
ISBN 0-915299-41-0 / 400 pages / $ 75.00 / Order code QFD-BK

Handbook of Quality Tools
The Japanese Approach
edited by Tetsuichi Asaka and Kazuo Ozeki

      The Japanese have stunned the world by their ability to produce top quality products at competitive prices. This comprehensive teaching manual, which includes the 7 traditional and 5 newer QC tools, explains each tool, why it's useful, and how to construct and use it. Information is presented in easy-to-grasp language, with step-by-step instructions, illustrations, and examples of each tool. A perfect training aid, as well as a hands-on reference book, for supervisors, foremen, and/or team leaders. Here's the best resource on the myriad Japanese quality tools changing the face of world manufacturing today. Accessible to everyone in your organization, dealing with both management and shop floor how-to's, you'll find it an indispensable tool in your quest for quality.
ISBN 0-915299-45-3 / 336 pages / $59.95 / Order Code HQT-BK

Productivity Press, Inc., Dept. BK, P.O. Box 3007, Cambridge, MA 02140 1-800-274-9911

The Battle to Stay Competitive
Changing the Traditional Workplace
The Delco Moraine NDH Story
by Charles Birkholz and Jim Villella

This inspiring and quick-reading book tells the story of one company's nontraditional response to increased competition and threatened market share. It recalls in vivid detail the changes undertaken by Delco Moraine NDH, General Motor's Brake Systems Division, that earned them a position as a world class supplier of automotive components. This case study documents the company's efforts to strengthen their competitiveness through synchronous manufacturing the coordination of resources (man, machine, and materials) to eliminate waste. The personal accounts of Charles Birkholz and Jim Villella, key players in the company's evolution, describe the various efforts at the floor level to change the standards and performance of their division of the decidedly traditional GM company.
ISBN 0-915299-96-8 / 208 pages / $9.95 / BATTLE-BK

Managerial Engineering
Techniques for Improving Quality and Productivity in the Workplace (rev.)
by Ryuji Fukuda

A proven path to managerial success, based on reliable methods developed by one of Japan's leading productivity experts and winner of the coveted Deming Prize for quality. Dr. W. Edwards Deming, world-famous consultant on quality, says that the book "provides an excellent and clear description of the devotion and methods of Japanese management to continual improvement of quality." (CEDAC training programs also available.)
ISBN 0-915299-09-7 / 208 pages / $39.95 / Order code ME-BK

The Visual Factory
Building Participation Through Shared Information
by Michel Greif

If you're aware of the tremendous improvements achieved in productivity and quality as a result of employee involvement, then you'll appreciate the great value of creating a visual factory. This book shows how visual management can be used to make the factory a place where workers and supervisors freely communicate and take improvement action. It details how to develop meeting and communication areas, communicate work standards and instructions, use visual production controls such as *kanban*, and make goals and progress visible. Over 200 diagrams and photos illustrate the numerous visual techniques discussed.
ISBN 0-915299-67-4 / 256 pages / $49.95 / Order Code VFAC-BK

Productivity Press, Inc., Dept. BK, P.O. Box 3007, Cambridge, MA 02140 1-800-274-9911

The Idea Book
Improvement Through Total Employee Involvement

Japan Human Relations Association (ed.)

What would your company be like if each employee — from line workers to engineers to sales people — gave 100 ideas every year for improving the company? This handbook of Japanese-style suggestion systems (called "teian"), will help your company develop its own vital improvement system by getting all employees involved. Train workers how to write improvement proposals, help supervisors promote participation, and put creative problem solving to work in your company. Designed as a self-trainer and study group tool, the book is heavily illustrated and includes hundreds of examples. (Spanish edition available.)
ISBN 0-915299-22-4 / 232 pages / $49.95 / Order code IDEA-BK

Canon Production System
Creative Involvement of the Total Workforce

compiled by the Japan Management Association

A fantastic success story! Canon set a goal to increase productivity by three percent per month — and achieved it! The first book-length case study to show how to combine the most effective Japanese management principles and quality improvement techniques into one overall strategy that improves every area of the company on a continual basis. Shows how the major QC tools are applied in a matrix management model.
ISBN 0-915299-06-2 / 251 pages / $36.95 / Order code CAN-BK

20 Keys to Workplace Improvement

by Iwao Kobayashi

This easy-to-read introduction to the "20 keys" system presents an integrated approach to assessing and improving your company's competitive level. The book focuses on systematic improvement through five levels of achievement in such primary areas as industrial housekeeping, small group activities, quick changeover techniques, equipment maintenance, and computerization. A scoring guide is included, along with information to help plan a strategy for your company's world class improvement effort.
ISBN 0-915299-61-5 / 264 pages / $34.95 / Order code 20KEYS-BK

Total Manufacturing Management
Production Organization for the 1990s

by Giorgio Merli

One of Italy's leading consultants discusses the implementation of Just-In-Time and related methods (including QFD and TPM) in Western corporations. The author does not approach JIT from a mechanistic orientation aimed simply at production efficiency. Rather, he discusses JIT from the perspective of industrial strategy and as an overall organizational model. Here's a sophisticated program for organizational reform that shows how JIT can be applied even in types of production that have often been neglected in the West, including custom work.
ISBN 0-915299-58-5 / 224 pages / $39.95 / Order code TMM-BK

Productivity Press, Inc., Dept. BK, P.O. Box 3007, Cambridge, MA 02140 1-800-274-9911

Introduction to TPM
Total Productive Maintenance
by Seiichi Nakajima

Total Productive Maintenance (TPM) combines the American practice of preventive maintenance with the Japanese concepts of total quality control (TQC) and total employee involvement (TEI). The result is an innovative system for equipment maintenance that optimizes effectiveness, eliminates breakdowns, and promotes autonomous operator maintenance through day-to-day activities. This book summarizes the steps involved in TPM and provides case examples from several top Japanese plants.
ISBN 0-915299-23-2 / 149 pages / $39.95 / Order code ITPM-BK

Achieving Total Quality Management
A Program for Action
by Michel Perigord

This is an outstanding book on total quality management (TQM) — a compact guide to the concepts, methods, and techniques involved in achieving total quality. It shows you how to make TQM a company-wide strategy, not just in technical areas, but in marketing and administration as well. Written in an accessible, instructive style by a top European quality expert, it is methodical, logical, and thorough. A historical outline and discussion of the quality-price relationship, is followed by an investigation of the five quality imperatives (conformity, prevention, excellence, measurement, and responsibility). Major methods and tools for total quality are spelled out and implementation strategies are reviewed.
ISBN 0-915299-60-7 / 384 pages / $39.95 / Order Code ACHTQM-BK

A Revolution in Manufacturing
The SMED System
by Shigeo Shingo, translated by Andrew P. Dillon

SMED (Single-Minute Exchange of Die), or quick changeover techniques, is the single most powerful tool for Just-In-Time production. Written by the industrial engineer who developed SMED for Toyota, the book contains hundreds of illustrations and photographs, as well as twelve chapter-length case studies. Here are the most complete and detailed instructions available anywhere for transforming a manufacturing environment to speed up production (Shingo's average setup time reduction is an astounding 98 percent) and make small-lot inventories feasible.
ISBN 0-915299-03-8 / 383 pages / $70.00 / Order code SMED-BK

The Improvement Book
Creating the Problem-Free Workplace
by Tomo Sugiyama

A practical guide to setting up a participatory problem-solving system in the workplace. Focusing on ways to eliminate the "Big 3" problems — irrationality, inconsistency, and waste — this book provides clear direction for starting a "problem-free engineering" program. It also gives you a full introduction to basic concepts of industrial housekeeping (known in Japan as 5S), two chapters of examples that can be used in small group training activities, and a workbook for individual use (extra copies are available separately). Written in an informal style, and using many anecdotes and examples, this book provides a proven approach to problem solving for any industrial setting.
ISBN 0-915299-47-X / 236 pages / $49.95 / Order code IB-BK

Productivity Press, Inc., Dept. BK, P.O. Box 3007, Cambridge, MA 02140 1-800-274-9911

Variety Reduction Program (VRP)
A Production Strategy for Product Diversification

by Toshio Suzue and Akira Kohdate

Here's the first book in English on a powerful way to increase manufacturing flexibility without increasing costs. How? By reducing the number of parts within each product type and by simplifying and standardizing parts between models. VRP is an integral feature of advanced manufacturing systems. This book is both an introduction to and a handbook for VRP implementation, featuring over 100 illustrations, for top manufacturing executives, middle managers, and R&D personnel.

ISBN 0-915299-32-1 / 164 pages / $59.95 / Order code VRP-BK

ALSO FROM PRODUCTIVITY

Productivity Newsletter

Productivity Newsletter has been helping America's most effective companies improve quality, lower costs, and increase their competitive power since 1979. Each monthly issue contains detailed case studies, articles on important innovations and world trends, book reviews, and much more. Subscribers save money on Productivity conferences and seminars. To subscribe, or for more information, call 1-800-888-6485. Please state order code "BA" when ordering.

TEI Newsletter

TEI — Total Employee Involvement — can transform an unproductive, inefficient, even angry work force into a smart, productive, cooperative team. Learn how by reading the monthly TEI Newsletter. Its articles, interviews, suggestions, and case histories will help you promote a learning organization, activate continuous improvement, and encourage creativity in all your employees. To subscribe, or for more information, call 1-800-888-6485. Please state order code "BA" when ordering.

Training Programs Available

Now you can learn for yourself just how to use the world's most powerful improvement process. We call it Continuous Systematic Improvement (CSI) using the CEDAC diagram. Both public workshops and dedicated in-house training are available to help you: o Develop reliable methods and procedures o Improve quality and productivity o Eliminate waste and lower costs o Involve employees at every level o Learn a fact-based, no-blame approach to continuous systematic improvement CSI and the CEDAC diagram will help you to solve problems permanently. Call 203-846-3777 today for free information about this remarkable program.

Productivity Press, Inc., Dept. BK, P.O. Box 3007, Cambridge, MA 02140 1-800-274-9911

COMPLETE LIST OF TITLES FROM PRODUCTIVITY PRESS

Akao, Yoji (ed.). **Quality Function Deployment: Integrating Customer Requirements into Product Design**
ISBN 0-915299-41-0 / 1990/ 387 pages / $ 75.00 / order code QFD

Asaka, Tetsuichi and Kazuo Ozeki (eds.). **Handbook of Quality Tools: The Japanese Approach**
ISBN 0-915299-45-3 / 1990 / 336 pages / $59.95 / order code HQT

Belohlav, James A. **Championship Management: An Action Model for High Performance**
ISBN 0-915299-76-3 / 1990 / 265 pages / $29.95 / order code CHAMPS

Christopher, William F. **Productivity Measurement Handbook**
ISBN 0-915299-05-4 / 1985 / 680 pages / $137.95 / order code PMH

D'Egidio, Franco. **The Service Era: Leadership in a Global Environment**
ISBN 0-915299-68-2 / 1990 / 165 pages / $29.95 / order code SERA

Ford, Henry. **Today and Tomorrow**
ISBN 0-915299-36-4 / 1988 / 286 pages / $24.95 / order code FORD

Fukuda, Ryuji. **CEDAC: A Tool for Continuous Systematic Improvement**
ISBN 0-915299-26-7 / 1990 / 144 pages / $49.95 / order code CEDAC

Fukuda, Ryuji. **Managerial Engineering: Techniques for Improving Quality and Productivity in the Workplace (rev.)**
ISBN 0-915299-09-7 / 1986 / 208 pages / $39.95 / order code ME

Hatakeyama, Yoshio. **Manager Revolution! A Guide to Survival in Today's Changing Workplace**
ISBN 0-915299-10-0 / 1986 / 208 pages / $24.95 / order code MREV

Hirano, Hiroyuki. **JIT Factory Revolution: A Pictorial Guide to Factory Design of the Future**
ISBN 0-915299-44-5 / 1989 / 227 pages / $49.95 / order code JITFAC

Hirano, Hiroyuki. **JIT Implementation Manual: The Complete Guide to Just-In-Time Manufacturing**
ISBN 0-915299-66-6 / 1990 / 1006 pages / $3500.00 / order code HIRANO

Horovitz, Jacques. **Winning Ways: Achieving Zero-Defect Service**
ISBN 0-915299-78-X / 1990 / 165 pages / $24.95 / order code WWAYS

Japan Human Relations Association (ed.). **The Idea Book: Improvement Through TEI (Total Employee Involvement)**
ISBN 0-915299-22-4 / 1988 / 232 pages / $49.95 / order code IDEA

Japan Human Relations Association (ed.). **The Service Industry Idea Book: Employee Involvement in Retail and Office Improvement**
ISBN 0-915299-65-8 / 1990 / 294 pages / $49.95 / order code SIDEA

Japan Management Association (ed.). **Kanban and Just-In-Time at Toyota: Management Begins at the Workplace (Revised Ed.),** Translated by
David J. Lu
ISBN 0-915299-48-8 / 1989 / 224 pages / $36.50 / order code KAN

Japan Management Association and Constance E. Dyer. **The Canon Production System: Creative Involvement of the Total Workforce**
ISBN 0-915299-06-2 / 1987 / 251 pages / $36.95 / order code CAN

Jones, Karen (ed.). **The Best of TEI: Current Perspectives on Total Employee Involvement**
ISBN 0-915299-63-1 / 1989 / 502 pages / $175.00 / order code TEI

Karatsu, Hajime. **Tough Words For American Industry**
ISBN 0-915299-25-9 / 1988 / 178 pages / $24.95 / order code TOUGH

Karatsu, Hajime. **TQC Wisdom of Japan: Managing for Total Quality Control,** Translated by David J. Lu
ISBN 0-915299-18-6 / 1988 / 136 pages / $34.95 / order code WISD

Kobayashi, Iwao. **20 Keys to Workplace Improvement**
ISBN 0-915299-61-5 / 1990 / 264 pages / $34.95 / order code 20KEYS

Lu, David J. **Inside Corporate Japan: The Art of Fumble-Free Management**
ISBN 0-915299-16-X / 1987 / 278 pages / $24.95 / order code ICJ

Merli, Giorgio. **Total Manufacturing Management: Production Organization for the 1990s**
ISBN 0-915299-58-5 / 1990 / 224 pages / $39.95 / order code TMM

Mizuno, Shigeru (ed.). **Management for Quality Improvement: The 7 New QC Tools**
ISBN 0-915299-29-1 / 1988 / 324 pages / $59.95 / order code 7QC

Monden, Yasuhiro and Michiharu Sakurai (eds.). **Japanese Management Accounting: A World Class Approach to Profit Management**
ISBN 0-915299-50-X / 1990 / 568 pages / $59.95 / order code JMACT

Nachi-Fujikoshi (ed.). **Training for TPM: A Manufacturing Success Story**
ISBN 0-915299-34-8 / 1990 / 320 pages / $59.95 / order code CTPM

Nakajima, Seiichi. **Introduction to TPM: Total Productive Maintenance**
ISBN 0-915299-23-2 / 1988 / 149 pages / $39.95 / order code ITPM

Nakajima, Seiichi. **TPM Development Program: Implementing Total Productive Maintenance**
ISBN 0-915299-37-2 / 1989 / 428 pages / $85.00 / order code DTPM

Nikkan Kogyo Shimbun, Ltd./**Factory Magazine (ed.). Poka-yoke: Improving Product Quality by Preventing Defects**
ISBN 0-915299-31-3 / 1989 / 288 pages / $59.95 / order code IPOKA

Ohno, Taiichi. **Toyota Production System: Beyond Large-Scale Production**
ISBN 0-915299-14-3 / 1988 / 162 pages / $39.95 / order code OTPS

Ohno, Taiichi. **Workplace Management**
ISBN 0-915299-19-4 / 1988 / 165 pages / $34.95 / order code WPM

Ohno, Taiichi and Setsuo Mito. **Just-In-Time for Today and Tomorrow**
ISBN 0-915299-20-8 / 1988 / 208 pages / $34.95 / order code OMJIT

Perigord, Michel. **Achieving Total Quality Management: A Program for Action**
ISBN 0-915299-60-7 / 1991 / 384 pages / $45.00 / order code ACHTQM

Psarouthakis, John. **Better Makes Us Best**
ISBN 0-915299-56-9 / 1989 / 112 pages / $16.95 / order code BMUB

Robson, Ross (ed.). **The Quality and Productivity Equation: American Corporate Strategies for the 1990s**
ISBN 0-915299-71-2 / 1990 / 558 pages / $29.95 / order code QPE

Shetty, Y.K and Vernon M. Buehler (eds.). **Competing Through Productivity and Quality**
ISBN 0-915299-43-7 / 1989 / 576 pages / $39.95 / order code COMP

Shingo, Shigeo. **Non-Stock Production: The Shingo System for Continuous Improvement**
ISBN 0-915299-30-5 / 1988 / 480 pages / $75.00 / order code NON

Shingo, Shigeo. **A Revolution In Manufacturing: The SMED System,** Translated by Andrew P. Dillon
ISBN 0-915299-03-8 / 1985 / 383 pages / $70.00 / order code SMED

Shingo, Shigeo. **The Sayings of Shigeo Shingo: Key Strategies for Plant Improvement, Translated by** Andrew P. Dillon
ISBN 0-915299-15-1 / 1987 / 208 pages / $39.95 / order code SAY

Shingo, Shigeo. **A Study of the Toyota Production System from an Industrial Engineering Viewpoint (rev.)**
ISBN 0-915299-17-8 / 1989 / 293 pages / $39.95 / order code STREV

Shingo, Shigeo. **Zero Quality Control: Source Inspection and the Poka-yoke System,** Translated by Andrew P. Dillon
ISBN 0-915299-07-0 / 1986 / 328 pages / $70.00 / order code ZQC

Shinohara, Isao (ed.). **New Production System: JIT Crossing Industry Boundaries**
ISBN 0-915299-21-6 / 1988 / 224 pages / $34.95 / order code NPS

Sugiyama, Tomo. **The Improvement Book: Creating the Problem-Free Workplace**
ISBN 0-915299-47-X / 1989 / 236 pages / $49.95 / order code IB

Suzue, Toshio and Akira Kohdate. **Variety Reduction Program (VRP): A Production Strategy for Product Diversification**
ISBN 0-915299-32-1 / 1990 / 164 pages / $59.95 / order code VRP

Tateisi, Kazuma. **The Eternal Venture Spirit: An Executive's Practical Philosophy**
ISBN 0-915299-55-0 / 1989 / 208 pages/ $19.95 / order code EVS

Audio-Visual Programs

Japan Management Association. **Total Productive Maintenance: Maximizing Productivity and Quality**
ISBN 0-915299-46-1 / 167 slides / 1989 / $749.00 / order code STPM
ISBN 0-915299-49-6 / 2 videos / 1989 / $749.00 / order code VTPM

Shingo, Shigeo. **The SMED System,** Translated by Andrew P. Dillon
ISBN 0-915299-11-9 / 181 slides / 1986 / $749.00 / order code S5
ISBN 0-915299-27-5 / 2 videos / 1987 / $749.00 / order code V5

Shingo, Shigeo. **The Poka-yoke System,** Translated by Andrew P. Dillon
ISBN 0-915299-13-5 / 235 slides / 1987 / $749.00 / order code S6
ISBN 0-915299-28-3 / 2 videos / 1987 / $749.00 / order code V6

TO ORDER: Write, phone, or fax Productivity Press, Dept. BK, P.O. Box 3007, Cambridge, MA 02140, phone 1-800-274-9911, fax 617-864-6286. Send check or charge to your credit card (American Express, Visa, MasterCard accepted).

U.S. ORDERS: Add $4 shipping for first book, $2 each additional for UPS surface delivery. CT residents add 8% and MA residents 5% sales tax.

INTERNATIONAL ORDERS: Write, phone, or fax for quote and indicate shipping method desired. Pre-payment in U.S. dollars must accompany your order (checks must be drawn on U.S. banks). When quote is returned with payment, your order will be shipped promptly by the method requested.

NOTE: Prices subject to change without notice.